ITALIAN
INTERMEZZO

BOOKS IN THE MENUS AND MUSIC SERIES

SHARON O'CONNOR'S MENUS AND MUSIC

ITALIAN INTERMEZZO

Recipes by
Celebrated Italian Chefs

Romantic Italian Music

Menus and Music Productions, Inc.
Emeryville, California

Remi recipes, pages 102 to 107, adapted with the permission of authors Adam D. Tihany, Florence Fabricant, and Peter Pioppo, from *Venetian Taste*, Abbeville Press, 1994.

Salsa Ericina recipe, page 212, adapted with the permission of author Carlo Middione, from *Carlo Middione's Traditional Pasta*, 10 Speed Press, 1996.

Excerpt from *The Complete Notebooks of Henry James*, Leon Edel and Lyall H. Powers, eds. Copyright 1986 by Leon Edel and Lyall H. Powers. Reprinted with the permission of Oxford University Press, Inc.

Excerpts from *A Room with a View*, by E.M. Forster. Reprinted with the permission of Alfred A. Knopf, a Division of Random House, Inc.

Excerpts from *The Enchanted April*, by Elizabeth Von Armin. Reprinted with the permission of Macmillan Press Ltd.

Excerpts from "Frutta Erbaggi" ("Fruits and Vegetables"), by Umberto Saba, translated by Henry Taylor, in *Poems from Italy*, New Rivers Press. 1985. Reprinted with the permission of Henry Taylor.

Excerpts from "Er Caffettiere Fisolofo" ("The Coffee House Philosopher"), by Giuseppe Gioacchino Belli, in *The Roman Sonnets of G.G. Belli*, translated by Harold Norse, Perivale Press, 1974. Reprinted with the permission of Lawrence Springarn and Perivale Press.

To the best of our knowledge, all other quotes used in this book are in the public domain. If we have neglected to obtain permission for any quotes that are still under copyright, please contact Menus and Music Productions, Inc., to ensure that the material is properly credited in the next edition.

Printed in Korea

Library of Congress Catalog Card Number: 00-102980

O'Connor, Sharon
Menus and Music Volume XV
Italian Intermezzo
  Recipes by Celebrated Italian Chefs
  Romantic Italian Music

Includes Index
1. Cookery 2. Entertaining
I. Title

ISBN 1-883914-22-1 (paperback with music compact disc)

Menus and Music Productions, Inc.
1462 66th Street
Emeryville, CA 94608
(510) 658-9100
Web Site: www.menusandmusic.com

Book and cover design: Fifth Street Design, Berkeley, CA
Food photographer: Paul Moore
Food stylist: Amy Nathan
Prop stylist: Sara Slavin

10 9 8 7 6 5 4 3 2 1

Contents

The sea
Which paves the desert streets of Venice laughs
In light and music . . .
—Percy Shelley, from "Ode to Naples"

INTRODUCTION

*". . . At least for me, I don't know how to think of
happiness, if I remove the pleasures of taste,
those of love, those of hearing,
and the delicate motions
that through sight I receive from forms . . ."*
—Epicuro

Enjoying a great home-cooked Italian dinner and glorious Italian songs in the midst of good company creates a glow of fundamental satisfaction. We don't notice cooking techniques or how the food looks on the plate—we just know that this is the way food is meant to be enjoyed. And we leave the table feeling better. The pleasure we receive is profound, because the impulse to create such a dinner comes from generosity and love. Remembrances of good home-cooked meals echo from generation to generation as an important part of the warm, secure embrace of family and home.

As a child, I ate my mother's cooking all week long, but every Saturday my father spent the better part of the day preparing the evening meal. This always entailed a trip to the local delicatessen, hours in the kitchen making everything from scratch, and the eagerly anticipated aroma of simmering sauces that made us hungry all afternoon. Dinner was by candlelight, always accompanied with music, and my brother and I got to celebrate with glasses of watered down wine. I am forever grateful that my Dad grew up in an Italian neighborhood!

While working on this project, I enjoyed cooking the following recipes in my own home kitchen; recording in New York beloved Italian songs that transport me to Italy, no matter where I hear them; traveling throughout Italy to interview great chefs and make sure that I correctly adapted their recipes for home cooks; and dining in extraordinary restaurant in Italy and the United States.

I'll always remember the day Carlo Brovelli promised "I'll cook for you tonight," and the parade of dishes that issued from Il Sole di Ranco's kitchen; a sensational dinner party at a private home in the hills near Asolo that was served in the garden under an arbor and accompanied by the antics of small dogs and choruses of laughter; Dottore Natale Rusconi bravely drawing me a gondola and Renato Picolotto generously showing me how to cook a few dishes in the Cipriani kitchen; dinner with my family on a floating deck and the mesmerizing beauty of Piazza San Marco bobbing in the distance while sensations became increasingly dreamlike; the irrepressibly good-humored Vittorio Dall'O in the garden at Villa San Michele joyfully arranging dinner plates in the flower beds for me to photograph; the day many pages of poems flew out our car window into the countryside somewhere between Florence and Siena; the overwhelming physical beauty of Alfonso and Livia Iaccarino's farm at the tip of the Sorrento peninsula, and actually hearing a gorgeous Italian woman exclaim *Mama mia!* every time she negotiated her tiny Fiat around a dramatic switchback while driving us to her farm, making me feel as though we might fall off Italy and onto the island of Capri.

It is my pleasure to present you with recipes from twenty-one of the very finest restaurants in Italy and the United States. I asked each chef to choose recipes with the home cook in mind that have been especially successful at his or her restaurant. Now, you can serve the same satisfying food at home. Most recipes are for everyday dishes, *piatti alla buona,* and some are *piatti domenicali,* Sunday dishes, to make when you have enough time to prepare a special meal. None of the recipes require cooking techniques that are beyond the skill of the average home cook.

You can re-create an entire menu from this book, choose dishes from several restaurants, or make just one of the recipes and serve it with your own favorites to make a balanced meal. Because the spirit of Italian cuisine is simplicity, it is perfect for cooking at home. In Italy, cooking is a family art, and the source of the best food is home kitchens, not restaurants. If you have limited time to prepare and enjoy a good meal, two cooks in the kitchen can have fun while saving a lot of time. Each cook can do what he or she likes and does best. For instance, my husband always rolls out the sheets of fresh pasta for ravioli while I make the sauce and filling. And remember: It's how the food tastes, not how it looks that counts. Of course using the finest-quality ingredients is fundamentally important, because Italian dishes are cooked simply to bring out the flavors of the ingredients, not to disguise or improve them.

Italians have long understood the joy of combining great food and music. Although La Scala in Milan is the haunt of music lovers, intellectuals, and socialites today, in previous centuries audiences combined opera with rather exuberant dining. The boxes had sitting rooms that were also used as dining rooms. Opera goers brought food with them that was warmed up on the premises by a restaurant established for that purpose, and on some occasions minestrone and veal steaks were served during performances. The great composer Berlioz complained that the music could hardly be heard over the clatter of knives and forks, although he did note that the noise usually ceased during the arias.

Italians may no longer dine in the opera house, but the enjoyment of good food and beautiful music is still integral to their flair for the art of living. Inspired by opera, Neapolitan songs have become popular worldwide thanks to Italian immigrants, pop singers, and operatic tenors. Irresistibly romantic, Italian songs are found in Hollywood movies, played as standards by jazz musicians, and, of course, essential at Italian wedding celebrations. The music recorded for this volume will set a joyous mood for you while cooking, during festive or romantic dining, and after wonderful meals. I've chosen songs that offer just a sample from the large body of Italian favorites. I know you'll enjoy the brilliant talent of guitarist Bucky Pizzarelli, clarinetist Ken Peplowski, mandolinist Lou Pallo, violinist Federico Britos, bassist Greg Cohen, and accordionist Charlie Giordano. Special thanks go to my friend Ken Peplowski for his artistry, for the arrangements, and for bringing the band together.

The food, music, and art of Italy have enriched the world for centuries, so including painting and poetry in this cookbook seemed entirely natural. Obviously Italians can't resist painting and writing about two of their great passions, so I was able to choose from abundant sources of paintings and poetry that highlight the affinity between food, music, and art.

When great Italian food and music are experienced together, the effect can be magical. I hope this volume inspires many evenings of music, food, joy, and romance in your home. *Buon appetito!*

—*Sharon O'Connor*

ITALIAN MENUS

Americans usually eat dinner with the meat, starch, and vegetables together on one plate, while Italian meals are served in courses that are brought to the table one at a time. Instead of having a main course, an Italian menu is composed of a sequence of dishes chosen to balance over the entire meal. The dishes vary with the seasons, but there is always a harmonious relationship between them.

Serving a meal in courses can make entertaining easier, since there's no need to have everything ready at once. Take your time while you add the finishing touches to the next course, allowing a few minutes for conversation, for refilling wineglasses, and for guests to relax and enjoy a leisurely meal. And, be sure to keep portions small so everyone can enjoy the many tastes of Italian cooking.

You might want to start your guests off with appetizers, or *antipasti*, to whet their appetites. In Italy, *antipasti* are served when entertaining and for special celebrations, but not usually before everyday family meals. Depending on your menu and the season, you could offer a platter of prosciutto with cantaloupe or figs, several varieties of salami with raw and marinated vegetables, Crostini with Chicken Livers (page 84), or Rosemary Spiedino of Seared Scallops (page 21).

The first course, or *primo piatto*, sets the pace for the rest of the meal and is usually a starch, such as pasta, risotto, or gnocchi, or a soup. The second course, or *secondo piatto*, almost always involves meat, poultry, or seafood (or a substantial vegetable dish or two for a vegetarian meal). The *secondo* is usually served with a *contorno*, a seasonal vegetable dish.

Green salads usually follow the second course, signaling the approaching finish of the meal. Everyday meals occasionally end with sweets, or *dolci,* but more typically with cheese and fresh fruit. Of course, a dessert is an anticipated part of family celebrations, holidays, and other important dinners. Italian meals usually end with espresso.

MUSIC NOTES

While recording the CD that accompanies this book, it was a privilege for me to work with guitarist Bucky Pizzarelli, clarinetist Ken Peplowski, mandolinist Lou Pallo, violinist Federico Britos, bassist Greg Cohen, and accordionist Charlie Giordano. Recording their brilliant talent during sessions in New York was an experience that I will remember always, and yes, we enjoyed eating Italian food together at the recording studio.

O Sole Mio
My Sunshine

Oh! what's so fine, dear, as a day of sunshine?
The sky is clear at last, the rain and storm are past,
Through air so cool, so bright, comes the festal sunlight.
Oh! What's so fine dear, as a day of sunsine?
        Another sunlight
            far lovelier lies
    Oh! my own sunshine,
    In your dear eyes
    Oh! my own sunshine
    In your dear eyes.

Arguably the best-loved of the Neapolitan songs, "O Sole Mio (My Sunshine)" was first heard in 1894 at an exhibition in the city of Milan. The gorgeous melody was composed by Eduardo di Capua (1864-1917) and is his hymn to the sun and the beauty of his beloved. The lyrics are by Giovanni Capurro (1859-1920).

Equally well known is "Santa Lucia (Over the Rippling Sea)," a traditional Neapolitan folk song arranged by Teodoro Cottrau (1827-1879). In the lyrics to this enchanting barcarole, an oarsman tries to persuade his love to board his boat and cross to beautiful Santa Lucia.

Tarantellas are Neapolitan dances in quick 6/8 meter and are probably named after the town of Taranto in southern Italy. When the joyfully energetic "Tarantella" recorded here is played at an Italian wedding celebration, the music usually accompanies a kind of mimed courtship dance performed by the newly wedded couple, who are surrounded by a circle of family and friends. The tarantula spider *(Lycosa tarentula)* also takes its name from the town of Taranto, which explains the widespread but discredited legend that the dance was created as a cure for the mildly toxic bite of the spider. In the mid-nineteenth century, classical composers such as Chopin, Liszt, Weber, and Gottschalk used tarantellas as virtuoso showpieces.

"Mattinata (You're Breaking My Heart)" is a lilting melody written for Enrico Caruso by Ruggero Leoncavallo (1857-1919), the Neapolitan composer whose fame rests on *Pagliacci*, his one celebrated opera. Leoncavallo wrote the lyrics and music for "Mattinata" and accompanied Caruso on the popular 1904 gramophone recording of the song. "Mattinata" was also a bestseller for tenor Beniamino Gigli as was "Torna a Surriento (Come Back to Sorrento)." This beloved melody was written in 1904 by Gigli's friend Ernesto De Curtis (1875-1937), and it is his most famous composition. De Curtis was Gigli's accompanist on concert tours and wrote numerous songs for the great tenor. The song's lyrics express the singer's plea that his love return to him and to the town of Sorrento. "Vieni sul Mar (Come to the Sea)," is a lovely Neapolitan folk song that has been recorded by many great tenors, including Enrico Caruso, Giuseppe di Stefano, and Luciano Pavarotti.

"Funiculì, Funiculà" was written in 1880 to commemorate the opening of the funicular rail to Vesuvius by Luigi Denza (1846-1922). A native

MUSIC NOTES

of Naples, Denza was a prominent and prolific composer of popular tunes; "Funiculì, Funiculà" is the best-known of his more than five hundred songs. In later life, Denza was a voice professor at the Royal Academy of Music in London.

"Arrivederci Roma (Goodbye to Rome)" was composed by Renato Rascel and featured in the 1958 Hollywood musical *Seven Hills of Rome*. The movie was filmed in Rome and stars the tenor Mario Lanza. "Anema e Core (With All My Heart and Soul)" by Salve d'Esposito was composed for the Italian film *Anema e Core* and has been recorded by a variety of artists, including Italian tenor Michelangelo Verso, singer Eddie Fisher, and jazz pianist Keith Jarrett. "Ciribiribin," a carefree Neapolitan waltz by Antonio Pestalozza first published in 1918, became a hit for the great swing orchestra of Harry James in the 1940s and 50s. The love song "Ah! Marie" by Eduardo di Capua was first published about 1899 with the title "Maria, Marì," and it has been recorded by a variety of famous singers, from Rosa Ponselle to Louis Prima.

ART NOTES

Giuseppe Arcimboldo (1527-93) Born in Milan, Arcimboldo began his career working for his father, Biagio Arcimboldo, who was also a painter. The younger Arcimboldo's first known works are designs for stained glass and tapestries. In 1562, he was called to be a court painter for Emperor Ferdinand I. He became a well-known figure at the royal court, and was connected with artistic and intellectual circles of his time.

Arcimboldo is most famous for his composite "heads": portraits created from an assembly of natural images including fruits, vegetables, and flowers. The paintings are rife with symbolic meanings, and can be seen as allegories of Habsburg glory (the Habsburg dynasty ruled central Europe from the thirteenth through the early twentieth centuries). Often connected to poems that provide clues to their symbolism, the use of wit and paradox in Arcimboldo's portraits is a typical Renaissance characteristic.

Canaletto (1697-1768) Canaletto was one of the first artists to depict the beauty of Venice. The painter, whose real name was Giovanni Antonio Canal, was trained to follow in his father's footsteps as a theatrical set designer. The first historical reference to young Canaletto in Venice occurs around 1720, when he helped his father design the sets for two Scarlatti operas. Canaletto soon turned from painting sets to painting canvases, but the artist's early training in perspective can be seen in his skill at rendering Venice's gorgeous palaces, monuments, and squares. Not surprisingly, his *vedute* (view paintings) were most popular among visitors to the city, particularly tourists from England.

Canaletto's sense of distance and proportion gives his paintings a sense of three-dimensional space and allows the viewer to enter into them almost as if they were real. In fact, modern-day historians and sociologists have studied Canaletto's work to learn about daily life in eighteenth-century Venice. His works influenced landscape painters for generations.

Caravaggio (1573-1610) Michelangelo Merisi was born into a family of landowners in a small community near Milan. When he moved to Rome as a young man, he took the name of his hometown: Caravaggio. A contemporary of Shakespeare, Galileo, and Monteverdi, Caravaggio rebelled against much of Italian and European artistic tradition. He lavished the same attention on still lifes as on figures, thus upsetting the hierarchy of the genres (in which historical painting came first). He is often quoted as having said that it gave him as much trouble to paint "a good picture of flowers as of figures." When he did paint portraits, Caravaggio exchanged idealism for frank realism, and he was one of the first artists to use commoners as models. The model for his *Bacchus*, for instance, was a young boy from the outskirts of Rome, rather than a nobleman as would have been traditional. Caravaggio's use of light was also innovative. In *Boy with a Basket of Fruit*, the light illuminating the boy's head and shoulders is obviously not from a real source. Instead, light is used as another element in the painting in order to emphasize certain details of the image. The figure and the splendid fruit basket in this painting compete equally for attention, which was an unconventional approach for its time.

Giacomo Ceruti (1698-1767) Ceruti's nickname was il Pitocchetto, after the beggars and vagabonds *(pitocchi)* he preferred to paint. Born in Milan, Ceruti moved to Brescia in 1721. Among his early patrons were wealthy Brescian families concerned about the social ills of their time. In the late 1720s, Ceruti began a series of works for the Avogardro family in which he used an objective, sensitive style to paint working people, the poor, beggars, and cripples. Influenced by Northern European painters, as well as contemporary Italian artists, Ceruti was part of a movement that used a direct, naturalistic style.

Giovanna Garzoni (1600-70) Garzoni specialized in paintings of fruit, vegetables, flowers, and animals, although she also painted portraits and devotional pictures. *Plate of Beans, Plate of Cherries and Carnations,* and *Fruit Dish with Pears and Cherries* are typical watercolors on parchment that focus on a fruit or vegetable. Her paintings combine the techniques of botanical illustration with attention to composition and design. Born in Ascoli Picena, Garzoni traveled throughout Italy during her career. She wrote to dal Pozzo that she wished to "live and die in Rome," and she eventually settled in that city in 1651. Garzoni was well respected in her time, and painted for members of the Medici court as well as for many patrons in Italy and Spain.

Jacopo Ligozzi (1547-1627) Ligozzi was born in Verona to a family of painters and designers of armor, tapestry, and silk embroidery. Around 1577, he moved to Florence, where he was employed by Grand Duke Francesco I. As was the case for many painters in the Medici court, Ligozzi's work was often more artisanal than artistic. For the Grand Duke, he painted birds, fish, plants and animals in a naturalist style. He also made drawings for objects in stained glass and for festival decorations, as well as drawings of allegories and religious scenes. Ligozzi's early training as a scientific draftsman can be seen in the precision and simplicity of his later works.

Francesco Malacrea (1812-86) Malacrea was born in the seaport city of Trieste in northeast Italy. He studied at the Academy of Art in Venice and was a painter of still lifes, flowers, and fruits. He is most famous for his murals, particularly his work on the ceiling of the Sartorio Palace in Trieste.

Cristoforo Munari (1667-1720) Known for his realistic details, Munari was primarily a painter of still lifes. The influence of Dutch painters can be seen in his interest and skill in painting reflective substances, such as glass. Munari was born in Reggio Emilia, where he lived until 1703. After three years of working for various members of the aristocracy in Rome, he moved to Florence, where he was a painter for the court of Ferdinand de' Medici. Eventually, Munari moved to Pisa and worked there as a painter and restorer of paintings until his death.

Cristoforo Rustici (1560-1640) Cristoforo Rustici was a member of the Rustici family of painters, who were based in Siena from the fifteenth through the seventeenth centuries. Little is known about the lives of these four generations of painters, which began with Cristoforo di Lorenzo Brazzi, Cristoforo Rustici's grandfather. The name Rustici comes from Lorenzo Brazzi's son, whose nickname was il Rustico (the rustic). Like his father, Cristoforo (also called il Rusticone) was known as a painter of frescoes, paintings made by applying water-based pigments directly onto freshly plastered walls while the plaster is still wet.

ANONYMOUS SEVENTEENTH CENTURY ITALIAN SCHOOL PAINTER.
Still Life with Flowers and Vegetables. Galleria Borghese, Rome, Italy

ACQUERELLO

San Francisco, California

Acquerello is an oasis of refinement, with crisp white tablecloths, large bouquets of fresh flowers, and watercolors of Venetian scenes and Palladian villas (*acquerello* means "watercolor" in Italian) softly illuminated by Murano lamps. The restaurant is an inspired collaboration between manager and wine expert Giancarlo Paterlini and chef Suzette Gresham-Tognetti, who coordinate their talents to provide a dining experience that is graceful, fresh, and spontaneous.

Suzette Gresham-Tognetti presents rich, deeply satisfying dishes, each with a creative touch: seasonal antipasti; silky housemade pastas with rustic sauces; nuanced and well-balanced main courses; and simple desserts with complex flavors, such as vanilla gelato drizzled with aged balsamic vinegar. Gresham-Tognetti enjoys developing recipes, and her creative reinventions of traditional regional dishes are perfectly cooked. Acquerello is known for its program of special dinners built around the wines of a certain region, as well as dinners that celebrate a single ingredient such as tomatoes, seafood, or the white truffle.

Often consulted as one of America's leading Italian wine experts, Bologna-born Paterlini buys the restaurant's Italian and California wines with Gresham-Tognetti's cooking in mind. If you wish, he will help you choose a different one for each course. In this way, diners can learn about wines while enjoying wonderful taste combinations they might not have discovered on their own. In 1997, *Wine Spectator* magazine placed Acquerello second on its list of America's ten best Italian restaurants. The following recipes were presented to Menus and Music by chef Suzette Gresham-Tognetti.

MENU

Rosemary Spiedino of Seared Scallops
with Balsamic Vinegar

Spiedino di Rosmarino con Capesante e Aceto Balsamico

Baby Spinach Salad with Olives, Ricotta Salata,
and Candied Walnuts

Insalata di Spinaci con Olive Nere e Noci Tostate

Shallot and Pancetta-Stuffed Filet of Beef
in Red Wine-Lavender Sauce

*Filetto di Manzo Ripieno con Pancetta e Scalogno
in Salsa di Lavanda*

Warm Zabaglione Scented
with Orange-Muscat Liqueur

Zabalione di Arancia al Moscato di Pantelleria

Sooth, the drinking should be ampler
When the drink is so divine
—Elizabeth Barrett Browning,
from "Wine of Cyprus"

■ Rosemary Spiedino of Seared ■ Scallops with Balsamic Vinegar

Spiedino di Rosmarino con Capesante e Aceto Balsamico

At Acquerello, chef Suzette Gresham-Tognetti uses flavorful rosemary branches to skewer the scallops. Wooden skewers soaked in warm water for 30 minutes work fine as well. When you make the pepper sauce ahead, this appetizer comes together in less than 15 minutes.

Rosemary-Balsamic Dressing

1 tablespoon balsamic vinegar

2 tablespoons extra-virgin olive oil

1 teaspoon minced fresh rosemary

¼ teaspoon minced garlic

1 teaspoon minced shallot

1 tablespoon minced fresh flat-leaf parsley

¼ teaspoon freshly ground pepper

½ teaspoon sugar

½ teaspoon salt

3 tablespoons extra-virgin olive oil

Six 10-inch-long (25-mm) straight fresh rosemary sprigs or wooden skewers

24 sea scallops

3 bunches fresh spinach, washed, stemmed, and dried

2 to 3 tablespoons balsamic vinegar

½ cup extra-virgin olive oil

2 tablespoons fresh lemon juice

Salt and freshly ground pepper to taste

Red Pepper Sauce (recipe follows)

To make the dressing: In a small bowl, whisk together all the ingredients; set aside.

If using the rosemary, leave about 1 inch (2.5 cm) of leaves at the tip of each rosemary branch and strip off the rest of the leaves. Using a sharp knife, cut the woody end of each sprig at an angle to make a point. Slide 4 scallops onto each sprig or skewer so the scallops will lie flat in the pan; set aside.

Preheat the oven to 450°F (230°C). Heat a large sauté pan or skillet over high heat until very hot. Add 2 tablespoons of the olive oil and sear the scallop skewers for 1 minute on each side, or until the scallops are golden on the outside but still translucent in the center. Remove from heat and discard the oil. Splash the scallops with balsamic vinegar. Transfer the skewers to a baking sheet and bake in the preheated oven for 2 to 3 minutes, or until the scallops are opaque throughout.

Meanwhile, in a large, heavy pan over medium-high heat, heat the remaining 1 tablespoon olive oil and swirl to coat the bottom. Add the spinach, cover, and shake in a circular motion for 2 minutes, or until the spinach is just wilted. Transfer the spinach to a colander; drain.

In a medium bowl, whisk the olive oil, lemon juice, salt, and pepper together. Add the spinach and toss well. Using tongs, place a nest of spinach in the center of each of 6 warmed plates and arrange a scallop skewer on top. Using a spoon or plastic squirt bottle, drizzle red pepper sauce decoratively around the perimeter of each plate. Brush the scallops with the rosemary-balsamic dressing and serve immediately.

Makes 6 servings

Red Pepper Sauce

1 tablespoon olive oil

1 shallot, minced

1 garlic clove, sliced

2 red bell peppers, seeded, deribbed, and chopped

½ cup (4 fl oz/125 ml) chicken broth (see Basics) or canned low-salt chicken broth

½ teaspoon fresh lemon juice

½ teaspoon salt

¼ teaspoon ground white pepper

In a small saucepan over medium heat, heat the olive oil and sauté the shallot and garlic for about 2 minutes, or until the shallot is translucent; do not brown. Add the bell peppers and sauté for 5 minutes, or until they soften and turn a lighter color. Pour in the broth and simmer for 20 minutes. Remove from heat and transfer to a food processor or blender. Add the lemon juice, salt, and pepper. Purée until smooth. Taste and adjust the seasoning.

Makes about 1 cup (8 fl oz/250 ml)

■ Baby Spinach Salad ■
with Olives, Ricotta Salata, and
Candied Walnuts

Insalata di Spinaci con Olive Nere e Noci Tostate

This remarkable combination of flavors creates a memorable salad. The candied walnuts can be made in advance and stored in an airtight container.

Candied Walnuts

¾ cup (3 oz/90 g) walnut halves and pieces

¼ cup (2 oz/60 g) sugar

8 handfuls baby spinach, washed, dried, and chilled

4 ounces (125 g) ricotta salata* cheese, finely sliced

¼ cup (2 oz/60 g) slivered red onions, rinsed and drained

Pitted brine-cured olives, such as gaeta or kalamata, for garnish (optional)

6 tablespoons (3 fl oz/80 ml) Olive Dressing (recipe follows)

Salt and freshly ground pepper to taste

To make the candied walnuts: In a small sauté pan or skillet over medium-high heat, toss the walnuts with the sugar for 3 to 4 minutes, or until the sugar melts and caramelizes; watch carefully, so the walnuts do not burn. Transfer the nuts to a lightly oiled plate or baking sheet and set aside to cool. Break apart any large clumps and chop coarsely.

In a large bowl, combine the spinach, ricotta salata, red onions, olives, olive dressing, and candied walnuts. Add the salt and pepper and toss gently.

Makes 6 servings

*Ricotta salata, a dry, aged version of fresh ricotta, is a salty, firm white sheep's milk cheese. Parmesan or pecorino may be used as a substitute. Ricotta salata is available at many cheese stores, specialty foods stores, and Italian markets.

Olive Dressing

For a salad dressing, this thick, chunky olive paste (tapenade) should be diluted with olive oil according to taste.

¼ cup (1 oz/30 g) pitted brine-cured black olives*

¼ cup (1 oz/30 g) mild California-style black olives, pitted

¼ cup (2 fl oz/60 ml) extra-virgin olive oil

¼ cup (2 fl oz/60 ml) pure olive oil

1 teaspoon minced shallot

¼ teaspoon minced garlic

1 tablespoon sherry vinegar

½ tablespoon sugar

Freshly ground pepper to taste

In a food processor, combine the two kinds of olives and pulse until finely chopped. In a nonaluminum bowl, whisk together the olives and all the remaining ingredients.

Makes 1 cup (8 fl oz/250 ml)

*Brine-cured black olives such as gaeta or kalamata are available at Italian markets. Other brine-cured ripe olives may be substituted.

Shallot and Pancetta-Stuffed Fillet of Beef

Filetto di Manzo Ripieno con Pancetta e Scalogni in Salsa di Lavanda

Sautéed Swiss chard is an excellent accompaniment for this stunning special-occasion dish. The rich red wine lavender sauce can be made ahead up to the point of reducing it to a final saucelike consistency, which can be done just before serving.

Filling

8 ounces (250 g) pancetta or bacon, chopped

½ cup (4 oz/125 g) chopped shallots

1 teaspoon minced garlic

½ cup (4 fl oz/125 ml) dry Marsala wine

5 tablespoons (3 oz/90 g) unsalted butter

Pinch of freshly ground pepper

1 tablespoon truffle peelings*

1 teaspoon truffle oil*

3 tablespoons minced fresh flat-leaf parsley

Red Wine-Lavender Sauce

1 teaspoon olive oil

2 unpeeled shallots, sliced

½ red onion, coarsely chopped

1 whole unpeeled garlic bulb, halved crosswise

1 celery stalk, coarsely chopped

1 unpeeled carrot, washed, scrubbed, and coarsely chopped

4 cups (1 l) dry red wine

1 cinnamon stick

1 tablespoon whole allspice

7 whole cloves

1⅓ cups (11 fl oz/330 ml) veal demi-glace*

½ teaspoon organic lavender flowers

6 thick fillet mignon steaks, about 5 ounces (155 g) each

2 tablespoons olive oil

Fresh organic lavender flowers for garnish (optional)

Sage leaves fried in butter for garnish (optional)

To make the filling: In a sauté pan or skillet over medium-high heat, sauté the pancetta or bacon for 2 minutes, or until it begins to render fat. Reduce heat to medium, add the shallot and garlic, and sauté for 2 minute. Pour in the Marsala, raise heat to medium-high, and cook to reduce by half. Add the butter, pepper, and truffle peelings and stir to melt the butter. Remove from heat and let cool. Transfer to a medium bowl and stir in the truffle oil and parsley. Cover the bowl with plastic wrap and refrigerate.

To make the sauce: In a large, heavy saucepan over medium heat, heat the olive oil and sauté the shallots, onion, garlic, celery, and carrot for 10 minutes. Stir in the red wine, cinnamon, allspice, and cloves. Reduce heat to low and simmer for 20 minutes. Add the veal demi-glace and lavender flowers and cook for another 10 minutes. Remove from heat and strain through a fine-meshed sieve; you should have about 1⅓ cups (11 fl oz/330 ml) of liquid. Just before serving, transfer to a saucepan and boil for 5 minutes to reduce to a saucelike consistency.

Insert the tip of a sharp knife into the side of each filet and sweep it around to make an internal pocket. Pull the knife back out at the point of entry, leaving as small a hole as possible. Using a demitasse or other small spoon, fill each beef pocket with about 1 tablespoon of the cooled pancetta mixture. Press down gently on the fillets; the beef should not be bulging. Season with salt and pepper.

Heat a large sauté pan or skillet over medium-high heat until very hot, add the olive oil, and brown the filets for 2 or 3 minutes on each side, for medium-rare.

To serve, ladle a pool of sauce onto each of 6 plates and arrange a filet in the center. Garnish with lavender flowers and fried sage leaves, if you wish.

Makes 6 servings

*Demi-glace, truffles, truffle peelings in olive oil, and truffle oil are available at Italian foods stores and other specialty foods stores. Also see Resources.

■ Warm Zabaglione ■
Scented with Orange-Muscat Liqueur
Zabaione di Arancia al Moscato di Pantelleria

Traditionally made with Marsala wine, Acquerello's version of zabaglione uses Moscato di Pantelleria, an elegant Italian dessert wine made from Muscat grapes.

2 oranges, peeled and segmented (see Basics)

2 tablespoons amaretti cookie crumbs

4 egg yolks

1½ tablespoons sugar

2 tablespoons Moscato di Pantelleria, Grand Marnier,
    or Triple Sec

¼ cup (2 fl oz/60 ml) dry white wine

Candied orange peel for garnish (see Basics for homemade)

Arrange the orange segments in 4 goblets or champagne glasses and sprinkle with the cookie crumbs.

In a double boiler over barely simmering water, whisk the egg yolks and sugar until frothy. Whisk in the Moscato or liqueur and white wine; whisk constantly until the mixture is light and fluffy and doubled in volume. It is important to whisk constantly or the yolks will cook and the mixture will curdle.

Spoon the zabaglione over the oranges, garnish with candied orange peel, and serve immediately.

Makes 4 servings

IL BOTTACCIO

Montignoso, Italy

Located less than two miles from the Ligurian Sea in the small town of Montignoso, Il Bottaccio is an elegant small hotel and superb restaurant created around an eighteenth-century water-powered olive oil press. (*Bottaccio* is the Italian word for the collection basin of the waters that turned the press.) Il Bottaccio offers an oasis of refinement and serenity, with antique furnishings, classic and contemporary Italian art, and a kitchen that delights even the most demanding palates. A member of the prestigious Relais & Chateaux Association, this is the perfect hotel for people who "don't like hotels" but prefer the tranquility and pleasures of the table found in a country house. Guests enjoy the fashionable beaches of Forte dei Marmi, hiking, tours of local vineyards, horseback riding, and visits to nearby Lucca and Pisa. Arrangements can be made for those who wish to commission a sculpture from the world-famous marble quarries of Carrara nearby.

Owners Elizabeth and Stefano D'Anna offer the hospitality of "a refined Tuscan villa where the pleasures of the table are harmonized with the savoring of comfort and calm." Blending styles and eras, they have decorated the hotel's public rooms and its eight luxurious suites with eighteenth-century Tuscan antiques, mosaics, and prestigious contemporary paintings and sculptures. Guests enjoy classical music during breakfast and excellent jazz during the afternoon.

A large indoor pool and a performance stage for musicians who perform during dinner are at the center of Il Bottaccio's restaurant, La Sala della Piscina. Here the food, music, and romantic setting conspire to create an atmosphere of unforgettable magic. The kitchen is overseen by Nino Mosca, who is an artistic, innovative chef inspired by Mediterranean tradition. Originally from Naples, Mosca continues to make use of the culinary skills he learned from his grandmother, who prepared large family meals every Sunday and taught her grandchildren to cook. Mosca enjoys developing new recipes, and his fish dishes are especially noteworthy. Each day the kitchen prepares a variety of fresh pastas, delicate pastries, and a fabulous selection of breads. The following recipes were presented to Menus and Music by chef Nino Mosca.

FRANCESCO MALACREA. Still Life with Fish and Mushrooms. Museo Civico Revoltella, Trieste, Italy

MENU

Oyster Ravioli with Sweet Pepper Sauce

Maccheroni di Ostriche in Salsa di Peperoni

Sea Bass with Zucchini Blossoms

Branzino ai Fiori di Zucca

Rolled Fillets of Sole with Porcini Mushroom Caps

Riccioli di Sogliola con Cappelle di Funghi Porcini

Honey Mousse with Struffoli

Mousse di Miele con Struffoli

◾ Oyster Ravioli ◾
with Sweet Pepper Sauce
Maccheroni di Ostriche in Salsa di Peperoni

A plate of velvet magic. The slightly smoky flavor of the roasted peppers beautifully complements the oysters. Bite-size pieces of steamed sea bass are an excellent substitute for the oysters.

Pasta

2½ cups (12½ oz/390 g) all-purpose flour

1 egg

3 egg yolks

3 dashes of salt

2 tablespoons olive oil

1 egg yolk beaten with 2 tablespoons water

Sauce

2 tablespoons olive oil

1 yellow bell pepper, roasted, peeled, and cut into very thin strips (see Basics)

1 red bell pepper, roasted, peeled, and cut into very thin strips (see Basics)

2 tablespoons heavy (whipping) cream

Salt to taste

Filling

2 tablespoons olive oil

12 small oysters, shucked

Splash of dry white wine

Salt and freshly ground pepper to taste

Chopped fresh flat-leaf parsley for garnish

To make the pasta: Pour the flour into a mound on a work surface and make a well in the center. Add the egg, egg yolks, salt, and olive oil to the well. Using a fork, beat the liquid ingredients just until blended. Begin mixing the flour into the eggs, drawing the flour from the inside wall of the well until a dough is formed. Alternatively, combine the ingredients in a food processor and process just until a ball is formed. On a floured work surface, knead the dough until smooth and elastic, about 8 minutes. Cut the dough into 4 equal sections, cover with plastic wrap, and let rest for 30 minutes before rolling out.

To make the filling: In a sauté pan or skillet over medium heat, heat the olive oil and sauté the oysters with the wine until firm. Season with salt and pepper and remove from heat.

To make the sauce: In a large sauté pan or skillet over medium heat, heat the olive oil, add the peppers, and toss. Stir in the cream and salt. Simmer for 5 minutes. Remove from heat. Cover and set aside.

Set the rollers of a pasta machine at the highest number. (The rollers will be wide apart.) Flatten one piece of dough into a rough rectangle. Feed the rectangle of pasta through the rollers. Fold the rectangle in half and feed through the rollers 8 or 9 more times, folding the dough in half each time and dusting it with flour if necessary to prevent sticking. Turn the dial down one notch and feed through the rollers without folding. Continue to feed through the rollers without folding, turning the dial one notch lower each time until the lowest or second-lowest notch is reached. The dough will be a smooth long sheet, 4 inches (10 cm) wide and about $1/16$ inch (2 mm) thick. Roll the remaining dough in same manner.

Cut the dough vertically into 2-inch-wide (5-cm) strips. Arrange the oysters on each strip, leaving a 1 inch (2.5 cm) border around each oyster. Brush the egg wash on the pasta around each oyster. Fold the dough in thirds lengthwise and close with light pressure. Using a pasta wheel or sharp knife, cut the ravioli and delicately separate.

In a large pot of salted boiling water, cook the ravioli for 3 minutes, or until they float to the top. Drain gently.

Meanwhile, reheat the sauce. Add the ravioli to the sauce and cook over medium heat for 1 or 2 minutes. Garnish with parsley and serve immediately

Makes 4 servings

■ Sea Bass with Zucchini Blossoms ■

Branzino ai Fiori di Zucca

If you grow zucchini in your garden, use the bright yellow-orange blossoms in this classic summer dish. Pick only male flowers that are still firmly closed. (Female flowers, which go on to produce the vegetables, have thicker stems than the males.) If zucchini blossoms are unavailable, substitute very thinly sliced zucchini.

3 tablespoons olive oil

16 to 24 zucchini blossoms, or 2 zucchini, very thinly sliced

4 sea bass fillets

Splash of dry white wine

Salt to taste

½ cup (4 fl oz/125 ml) fish stock (see Basics) or canned low-salt chicken broth

4 deep-fried zucchini blossoms for garnish (optional), see Basics

Preheat the oven to 400°F (200°C). In a large ovenproof sauté pan or skillet over medium heat, heat the olive oil and sauté the blossoms or zucchini slices for 2 minutes. Using a slotted spoon, transfer the blossoms or zucchini slices to a plate. Arrange the sea bass, skin-side down, in the pan and add the white wine and salt. Top the fish with the blossoms or zucchini slices, raise heat to high, and cook for 2 minutes. Pour in the stock or broth. Transfer to the preheated oven and bake for 5 minutes, or until the fish is opaque throughout.

Arrange a fish fillet topped with blossoms or zucchini slices on each of 4 warmed plates and drizzle the sauce over. Garnish with a fried zucchini blossom, if desired, and serve immediately.

Makes 4 servings

■ Rolled Fillets of Sole ■ with Mushroom Caps

Riccioli di Sogliola con Cappelle di Funghi

This fanciful dish blends the flavors of the forest and the sea: Whole mushroom caps top rolled fish fillets set on end to resemble mushroom stems.

6 sole fillets, halved lengthwise

3 tablespoons olive oil

12 small porcini or cremini mushrooms, stemmed

Salt to taste

¼ cup (2 fl oz/60 ml) fish stock (see Basics) or canned low-salt chicken broth

½ cup (4 fl oz/125 ml) dry white wine

1 fresh mint sprig

Sprigs of fresh mint or lemon verbena for garnish

Preheat the oven to 400°F (200°C). Roll the sole fillets into 12 tight cylinders and secure each one with 3 toothpicks.

In a medium ovenproof sauté pan or skillet over medium heat, heat the olive oil and sauté the mushroom caps until lightly browned. Season with salt and add the stock or broth. Transfer the pan to the oven and bake for 5 minutes.

Meanwhile, in a large ovenproof sauté pan or skillet, combine the wine, mint, and sole. Cook over medium heat to reduce the wine until almost evaporated. Sprinkle the fish with salt. Transfer the pan to the preheated oven and bake for 3 minutes, or until the fish is opaque throughout, adding more stock or broth if needed. Transfer the fish to a plate, cover, and set aside.

Transfer the mushrooms and their cooking juices to the pan with the sole and cook over high heat to reduce. Carefully remove the toothpicks from the fish. Arrange 3 fish rolls on each of 4 hot plates so they stand upright. Top each curl with a mushroom cap to simulate a whole mushroom. Spoon a little sauce over, garnish with mint or lemon verbena, and serve immediately.

Makes 4 servings

■ Honey Mousse with Struffoli ■

Mousse di Miele con Struffoli

A traditional Christmas sweet from southern Italy, served with a creamy mousse. Struffoli are deep-fried pastry cubes that are bathed in honey and sprinkled with brightly colored sugar to recall the confetti of Carnevale.

Honey Mousse

6 eggs

2 tablespoons sugar

¼ cup (2 fl oz/60 ml) water

1 envelope plain gelatin

¼ cup (3 oz/90 g) flavorful honey, or to taste

1⅓ cups (11 fl oz/330 ml) heavy (whipping) cream, beaten until soft peaks form

Struffoli

1½ cups (7½ oz/235 g) plus 1 tablespoon all-purpose flour

3 tablespoons sugar

¼ teaspoon baking soda

2 tablespoons butter, melted

3 eggs

2 tablespoons rum

3 tablespoons grated orange zest (see Basics)

1 tablespoon grated lemon zest (see Basics)

Vegetable oil for deep-frying

¾ cup (9 oz/280 g) honey

Colored sugar sprinkles for garnish

To make the mousse: In a large bowl, beat the eggs with the sugar until thick and foamy.

Add the water to a small saucepan and sprinkle in the gelatin; let soak for 1 minute. Stir over low heat until the gelatin is completely dissolved.

Remove from heat, stir in the honey, and let cool slightly. Stir the gelatin mixture into the egg mixture until blended. Fold in the whipped cream. Cover and refrigerate for at least 3 hours.

To make the struffoli: Sift the flour, sugar, and baking soda together onto a pastry board. Make a well in the center of the flour mixture and add the eggs, butter, and rum. Use a fork to beat the eggs, butter, rum, and zest until blended. Gradually beat in the flour, beginning with the inside of the well, until a dough is formed. Alternatively, combine the flour, butter, eggs, rum, and zest in a food processor and process just until the mixture forms a ball.

On a lightly floured work surface, roll out the dough to a ¼-inch (6-mm) thickness and sprinkle with flour. Using a sharp knife, cut the dough into ¼-inch-wide (6-mm) strips and cut the strips into ¼-inch (6-mm) squares.

In a Dutch oven or deep fryer, heat 3 inches (7.5 cm) vegetable oil to 350°F (180° C), or until a piece of dough frizzles and blisters when dropped into the oil. Working in batches, slip the struffoli into the oil and fry for 45 to 60 seconds, or until golden. Using a wire-mesh skimmer or slotted spoon, transfer the struffoli to paper towels to drain. Transfer to a buttered plate, drizzle with the honey, and let cool for 5 minutes. Moisten your hands with water and shape the struffoli into 6 mounds. Arrange a struffoli mound on each of 6 plates and sprinkle with colored sugar. Serve with a scoop of honey mousse alongside.

Makes 6 to 8 servings

CRISTOFORO RUSTICI. October from 'Six Months of the Year'. Museo Civico, Siena, Italy

For July, in Siena, by the willow-tree,
    I give you barrels of white Tuscan wine
    In ice far down your cellars stored supine;
And morn and eve to eat in company
Of those vast jellies dear to you and me;
Of partridges and youngling pheasants sweet...

—Folgore da San Geminiano
from "Of the Months: Twelve Sonnets
Addressed to a Fellowship of Sienese Nobles"

    Grape-harvest began.
In the vat, halfway up in our house-side,
    Like blood the juice spins,
While your brother all bare-legged is dancing
    Till breathless he grins
Dead-beaten in effort on effort
    To keep the grapes under,
Since still when he seems all but master,
    In pours fresh plunder
From girls who keep coming and going
    With basket on shoulder

—Robert Browning,
from "The Englishman in Italy"

HOTEL CERTOSA DI MAGGIANO

Siena, Italy

Originally built in 1314 by order of Cardinal Riccardo Petroni, Hotel Certosa di Maggiano is a former Carthusian monastery. Situated in the Tuscan countryside, this small luxury hotel is less than two miles from the medieval city of Siena, with its magnificent cathedral and Piazza del Campo, scene of the famous Palio, the city's bareback horse race. After six years of careful restoration, Certosa di Maggiano was opened in 1975 by Anna Recordati, and today she manages the hotel with her daughter, Margherita Grossi. On entering the property's walled enclave, visitors step into a strikingly austere courtyard with open galleries and an original stone well. The hotel's seventeen comfortable rooms overlook a pastoral scene of vineyards, olive groves, arbors, and abundant kitchen gardens. Guests can enjoy the library and game room and a sitting room with open fireplace, as well as strolling in the thirty-acre garden and swimming in the heated outdoor pool. The breakfast room nestles comfortably within an old Tuscan kitchen that opens onto an arbor-covered patio. Arrangements can be made for special cooking and photography classes; private tours of Siena, Chianti vineyards, and castles; tickets for Palio races or dinner in Siena's various contrada during the Palio season; and tickets for classical music concerts at the Accademia Chigiana.

Il Canto, Certosa's elegant dining room, is furnished with a collection of majolica (richly decorated glazed Italian pottery) and lit by a gorgeous Murano chandelier. During summer months, guests can enjoy alfresco dining by candlelight in the arcade of the courtyard. The superb menu offers seasonal selections of Tuscan cuisine and fine wines of the region.

MENU

Savory Bread Salad

Panzanella

Pasta with Rabbit Sauce

Pici alla Senese

Roast Guinea Hen with Fonduta

Faraona Arrosto con Fonduta

Tuscan Bread Pudding with Mascarpone
and Almond Sauce

Budino di Pane con Mascarpone e Mandorle

■ Savory Bread Salad ■
Panzanella

Serve this traditional Tuscan summer salad as a first course at the peak of tomato season, with olive oil and vinegar at the table so that each person can season to taste.

1 loaf day-old Italian or French bread, crusts removed, sliced

3 tomatoes, peeled, seeded, and cut into ½-inch (12-mm) chunks (see Basics)

1 red onion, thinly sliced

½ small cucumber, peeled and thinly sliced

⅓ cup (3 fl oz/80 ml) extra-virgin olive oil, plus more to taste

Salt and freshly ground pepper to taste

½ cup (⅔ oz/20 g) coarsely chopped fresh basil, plus fresh basil sprigs for garnish

2 tablespoons red wine vinegar

Tomato slices for garnish

Put the bread slices in a medium bowl and add cold water to cover. Soak for 10 minutes, or until the bread is spongy. Using your hands, gently squeeze out all the water. Rub the bread between your palms to make coarse crumbs.

In a large bowl, combine the bread crumbs, tomatoes, onion, cucumber, ⅓ cup (3 fl oz/80 ml) olive oil, salt, pepper, and chopped basil. Gently toss the salad with your hands. Cover and set aside for at least 30 minutes. Just before serving, toss with the vinegar and more olive oil to taste. Garnish with tomato slices and basil sprigs.

Makes 4 servings

HOTEL CERTOSA DI MAGGIANO

▪ Pasta with Rabbit Sauce ▪
Pici alla Senese

Pici is a fresh Tuscan pasta similar to a thick spaghetti. If you don't have time to make it, this sauce is equally good with either fresh or dried pappardelle, also traditionally served with rabbit sauce. Rabbit has a lean meat with a delicate flavor and is popular in Italy. The sauce may be prepared the day before you plan to serve it. Cover, refrigerate, and bring to a simmer over low heat just before serving.

Rabbit Sauce

2 tablespoons olive oil

1 onion, chopped

1 celery stalk, chopped

3 carrots, peeled and chopped

1 pound (500 g) rabbit loin, coarsely chopped (see Resources)

⅓ rabbit liver, diced (optional)

½ cup (4 fl oz/125 ml) dry white wine

1 pound (500 g) Roma (plum) tomatoes, peeled, seeded, and coarsely chopped (see Basics)

Mixed chopped fresh rosemary and thyme to taste

Salt and freshly ground pepper to taste

Pasta

About 1½ cups (7½ oz/230 g) plus 1 tablespoon all-purpose flour

3 eggs

¼ cup (2 fl oz/60 ml) extra-virgin olive oil

Pinch of salt

¼ cup (1 oz/30 g) freshly grated Parmesan cheese

⅓ cup (½ oz/15 g) minced fresh flat-leaf parsley

To make the sauce: In a large sauté pan or skillet over medium heat, heat the olive oil and sauté the onion, celery, and carrots for 10 minutes. Raise

heat to medium-high, add the rabbit and liver, and cook for 10 minutes, stirring occasionally. Pour in the wine and cook for 20 minutes, or until most of the wine evaporates.

Stir in the tomatoes, rosemary, and thyme. Simmer over medium heat for 30 minutes. Season with salt and pepper. Set aside and keep warm.

To make the pasta: Pour the flour into a mound on a work surface and make a well in the center. Add the eggs, olive oil, and salt. Using a fork, beat the eggs and oil until blended. Begin mixing the flour into the egg mixture, drawing the flour from the inside wall of the well, until a dough is formed. Add more flour, 1 tablespoon at a time, if the dough is sticky. Alternatively, combine the flour, eggs, olive oil, and salt in a food processor and process until the mixture just forms a ball. If the dough is sticky, add more flour, 1 tablespoon at a time, and process after each addition to make a smooth dough.

On a lightly floured work surface, knead the dough until smooth, about 8 minutes. Cover with plastic wrap and let rest for at least 30 minutes.

Form the dough into walnut-sized balls and roll each ball into a cigar-shaped log. Using the palm of the right hand, press down on each log while rolling it out on the lightly floured surface. Pull on the opposite end of the log with the left hand; the log will increase in length until it is about 16 inches (40 cm) long. Place the pasta on a kitchen towel and sprinkle with flour or cornmeal to prevent sticking. Repeat the steps with the remaining dough. Let dry for 30 minutes. Cut each strand in half to create pieces about 8 inches (20 cm) long.

Just before serving, cook the pasta in a large pot of salted boiling water until al dente, 2 to 3 minutes. Transfer the pasta to a large warmed pasta bowl. Add the rabbit sauce and quickly toss to coat thoroughly. Sprinkle with the Parmesan cheese and parsley. Serve immediately.

Makes 4 servings

Roast Guinea Hen with Fonduta

Faraona Arrosto con Fonduta

In Italy, robust-flavored guinea hen is prepared much the same way as chicken. At Ristorante Il Canto, roasted guinea hen is served with a creamy cheese sauce of melted Tuscan pecorino, a fairly mild sheep's milk cheese. Fontina cheese may also be used. A small chicken or 2 Cornish hens may be substituted for the guinea hen.

Salt and freshly ground pepper to taste

One guinea hen (about 2 pounds), giblets removed

1 fresh rosemary sprig

2 garlic cloves

2 tablespoons extra-virgin olive oil

1/2 cup (4 fl oz/125 ml) dry red wine

Fonduta

3 tablespoons butter

1/4 cup (1 1/2 oz/45 g) flour

2 cups (16 fl oz/500 ml) beef broth (see Basics) or canned low-salt beef broth

5 ounces (155 g) Tuscan pecorino cheese, thinly sliced

Salt and freshly ground pepper to taste

Preheat the oven to 350°F (180°C). Salt and pepper the hen inside and out. Place the rosemary and garlic inside the body cavity and truss with string.

In a large, heavy ovenproof skillet or heavy roasting pan over medium-high heat, heat the olive oil and quickly brown the hen on all sides. Pour the red wine over. Roast in the preheated oven, basting periodically, for 1 hour and 45 minutes, or until the juices run clear when a knife is inserted in the thickest part of the thigh. Remove the trussing string.

Meanwhile, prepare the fonduta: In a medium saucepan, melt the butter over medium-low heat and stir in the flour; stir for 2 or 3 minutes. Whisk in the broth and cook, stirring frequently, for about 10 minutes. Add the cheese, salt, and pepper and stir until the cheese melts. Cut the hen into quarters, spoon over the hot fonduta, and serve.

Makes 4 servings

▪ Tuscan Bread Pudding ▪ with Mascarpone and Almond Sauce

Budino di Pane con Mascarpone e Mandorle

This scrumptious bread pudding can be made 3 or 4 days ahead and stored in the refrigerator. Serve warm or at room temperature.

2 egg yolks

½ cup (4 oz/125 g) sugar

2 cups (16 fl oz/500 ml) milk

3 tablespoons apricot or strawberry jam

3 tablespoons (2 oz/60 g) honey

⅓ cup (2 oz/60 g) golden raisins

½ loaf day-old Italian or French bread (without crusts), sliced into thin strips

Mascarpone and Almond Sauce (recipe follows)

Butter an 8-inch (20-cm) square baking dish. Preheat the oven to 350°F (180°C).

In a medium bowl, beat the egg yolks and sugar together. Whisk in the milk, jam, and honey. Stir in the raisins.

Arrange the bread slices in the bottom of the prepared baking dish. Pour the custard mixture evenly over the bread, moistening every slice. Let stand for 15 minutes.

Set the baking dish in a large baking pan and fill the pan with water to reach halfway up the sides of the baking dish. Bake in the preheated oven for about 40 minutes, or until a knife inserted in the center comes out clean. Cut into slices and serve on dessert plates with a dollop of sauce.

Makes 6 servings

Mascarpone and Almond Sauce

⅓ cup (1½ oz/50 g) unblanched almonds

1 egg yolk

¼ cup (2 oz/60 g) sugar

5 ounces (155 g) mascarpone cheese* at room temperature

In a food processor, pulse the almonds until ground.

In a medium bowl, beat the egg yolk and sugar together. Whisk in the mascarpone until fluffy. Stir in the ground almonds.

Makes about 1 cup

*Mascarpone, a delicately flavored triple-cream cheese from Lombardy, is usually sold in plastic containers and is available in many grocery stores and most Italian foods stores.

Note: If you are concerned about eating uncooked eggs, do not make this recipe.

GIOVANNI ANTONIO CANALETTO. View of the Ducal Palace. Uffizi, Florence, Italy

Venice glowed and plashed and called and chimed again; the air was like a clap of hands, and the scattered pinks, yellows, blues, sea-greens, were like a hanging-out of vivid stuffs, a laying-down of fine carpets.

—Henry James, *The Wings of the Dove*

HOTEL CIPRIANI

Venice, Italy

When Commendator Giuseppe Cipriani, the legendary restaurateur and founder of Venice's Harry's Bar, opened the doors of the Cipriani Hotel to instant acclaim in 1958, he realized his dream of creating a hotel within easy reach of Piazza San Marco yet far enough away to guarantee peace and privacy. Guests cross the fabled lagoon to the island of Giudecca in the Cipriani's sleek motor launch to find fine cuisine, resplendent accommodations, gardens with a heated Olympic-size saltwater swimming pool, and loggias and walks that provide the relaxed atmosphere of a country estate. The hotel's annex, Palazzo Vendramin, is a fifteenth-century palace linked to the hotel through an ancient courtyard and has the atmosphere of a luxurious private home. The restored sixteenth-century Palazzetto Nani Barbaro offers five fabulous suites with breathtaking views of the Venetian skyline. On the ground floor of the Palazzetto is Cip's, a restaurant, pizzeria, grill, and dolci bar all in one. Cip's floating wooden terrace looks towards Piazza San Marco, Venice's sumptuous outdoor salon, and dining here while a guitarist serenades is a sublime experience.

Dottore Natale Rusconi, the Cipriani's managing director since 1977, is renowned in the hospitality business. A culinary expert, he introduced cooking schools to Italy at the suggestion of his friend, James Beard. Today the Cipriani's cooking classes feature leading chefs such as Julia Child, Marcella Hazan, Anne Willan, and Faith Willinger. The classes include feasts at the hotel, dinner parties in nearby palazzos, olive oil and grappa tastings, visits to the Rialto market and other landmarks, and even a Venetian masked ball.

Executive chef Renato Piccollotto creates superb classic and creative Venetian dishes that are served with a style that is legendary. The Cipriani's wine list is focused yet comprehensive, and wines are categorized to make the list user-friendly. Dining in the Venetian room, with its Murano chandeliers and Fortuny curtains, or alfresco in the splendid waterside Terrace restaurant at twilight, is the embodiment of romance. Luncheon is served poolside, and the lavish breakfast buffet includes a choice of croissants and brioche, fabulous omelettes, Italian cheeses, Parma ham, fresh fruits, juices, and espresso. Thus fortified, guests have more than enough energy for exploring Venice, with its network of bridges and canals, architectural monuments, art galleries, and museums, including the Galleria dell'Academia, with Venetian masterpieces from the fourteenth to eighteenth centuries, and the Peggy Guggenheim Collection, one of the world's finest collections of twentieth-century art.

After spending sessions with chef Renato Piccolotto in the Cipriani kitchen, it was soon apparent that he is a perfectionist, a joyfully creative chef, and a remarkably patient and generous man. Chef Piccolotto visits the Rialto market most mornings to ensure quality and to monitor seasonal produce and seafood. The bustling Rialto district was the site of Venice's first settlement and has been the city's commercial center for centuries. Once a grand bazaar for spices, jewels, and silks from the Orient, it is now a colorful food market where all of Venice comes to do its shopping. Chef Renato Piccolotto presented Menus and Music with the following recipes.

HOTEL CIPRIANI

The lovely Venetian spring came and went, and brought with it an infinitude of impressions, of delightful hours. I became passionately fond of the place, of the life, of the people, of the habits. I asked myself at times whether it wouldn't be a happy thought to take a little pied-à-terre there, which one might keep forever.

—Henry James,
The Complete Notebooks of Henry James

HOTEL CIPRIANI

MENU

Thinly Sliced Raw Prime Beef with Cipriani Sauce
Carpaccio Cipriani

Monkfish Medallions with Tomatoes and Olives
Medaglioni di Coda di Rospo ai Filetti de Pomodoro e Olive

Surprise of the Sea
Sorpresa di Mare

Venetian Tiramisù with Vanilla Sauce
Tiramisù alla Veneziana con Salsa alla Vaniglia

■ Thinly Sliced Raw Prime Beef ■ with Cipriani Sauce

Carpaccio Cipriani

This dish was created in the early 1960s by Giuseppe Cipriani and served as the first course for a banquet at the Hotel Cipriani to mark the opening of a great exhibition of paintings by Carpaccio. Cipriani's dish of paper-thin slices of beef with mustard-spiked mayonnaise was inspired by the reds and yellows often used by the fifteenth-century Venetian painter.

Dr. Natale Rusconi, managing director of the Cipriani, suggests that the meat used for this recipe should be cut from the sirloin rather than the fillet. Chilling the meat makes it easier to slice, but it should not be cut when completely frozen, as this can cause puddles of water to form on the plate.

12 ounces (375 g) prime rib steak (sirloin, not fillet)

Cipriani Sauce

1 cup (8 oz/250 g) mayonnaise (see Basics for homemade)

1 tablespoon Worcestershire sauce

½ teaspoon Colman's dry mustard

1 tablespoon fresh lemon juice

Few drops of Tabasco sauce

Salt and freshly ground pepper to taste

⅓ cup (3 fl oz/80 ml) reduced beef broth (see Basics)

Cover the meat with plastic wrap and place it in the freezer until nearly frozen, 2 to 3 hours. Cut across the grain into paper-thin slices. If your butcher slices the beef, use the meat on the same day, or it may discolor.

To make the sauce: In a medium bowl, mix the mayonnaise, Worcestershire sauce, mustard, lemon juice, Tabasco, salt, and pepper together until well blended. Stir in the broth. Cover and refrigerate until chilled, at least 1 hour.

Arrange the sliced meat on each of 4 chilled plates so the meat completely covers the plate. Drizzle the sauce over in a spiral pattern, starting from the center, and create a decorative design by running a fork through the sauce. Serve immediately.

Makes 4 servings

■ Monkfish Medallions ■ with Tomatoes and Olives

Medaglioni di Coda di Rospo ai Filetti de Pomodoro e Olive

If monkfish is unavailable, substitute sea bass or turbot. Serve this luxurious yet quickly prepared dish with boiled or steamed new potatoes.

3 tablespoons olive oil

2 tablespoons julienned leek

¼ cup (1 oz/30 g) julienned carrot

¼ cup (1 oz/30 g) julienned celery

4 monkfish fillets, quartered

Salt and freshly ground pepper to taste

2 cups (16 fl oz/500 ml) dry white wine

⅓ cup (3 fl oz/80 ml) fish stock (see Basics) or canned low-salt chicken broth

20 brine-cured black olives, pitted and cut into strips

2 Roma (plum) tomatoes, peeled, seeded, and sliced lengthwise into thin strips (see Basics)

4 fresh basil leaves, plus basil sprigs for garnish

1½ tablespoons butter

Virgin olive oil for drizzling

In a large sauté pan or skillet over medium heat, heat 1 tablespoon of the olive oil and sauté the leek, carrot, and celery for 2 or 3 minutes.

In a large sauté pan or skillet over medium-high heat, heat the remaining 2 tablespoons olive oil and sauté the fish for 1 or 2 minutes on each side, or just until golden. Season with salt and pepper. Stir in the sautéed vegetables, wine, and stock or broth; cover the pan and cook for 3 minutes. Add the olives, tomatoes, shredded basil, butter, and a generous drizzle of olive oil; cook for 2 minutes. Season with salt and pepper.

Arrange 4 pieces of fish on each of 4 warmed plates. Ladle the vegetables and sauce over. Garnish with the basil sprigs and serve immediately.

Makes 4 servings

■ Surprise of the Sea ■
Sorpresa di Mare

*An assortment of fish and shellfish baked under a golden pastry crust.
When served, the pastry is inverted and filled with the seafood.*

Pastry Dough

⅓ cup (3 oz/90 g) cold unsalted butter, cut into small pieces

1 small egg yolk

½ teaspoon salt

¼ cup (2 fl oz/60 ml) cold water

1¼ cups (6½ oz/220g) all-purpose flour

1 monkfish, sea bass, or turbot fillet, cut into bite-sized pieces

4 small fillets of sole, quartered

4 scampi, prawns, or large shrimp, shelled and deveined

4 sea scallops

8 littleneck clams, shucked

Extra-virgin olive oil for drizzling

1 tablespoon chopped pine nuts

1 tablespoon finely chopped almonds, toasted (see Basics)

½ garlic clove, minced

2 tablespoons minced fresh flat-leaf parsley

¼ cup (2 fl oz/60 ml) dry white wine

Fresh lemon juice to taste

Salt and freshly ground pepper to taste

4 fresh basil leaves

Pastry Dough (recipe follows)

1 egg, beaten

Cumin or caraway seeds for sprinkling

To make the dough: In a food processor, combine the butter, egg yolk, and salt and process until the mixture resembles coarse crumbs, about 15 seconds. With the machine running, add the water in a steady stream and process until the dough just forms a ball, about 20 seconds. Flatten the dough into a disk, enclose in plastic wrap, and refrigerate for at least 30 minutes.

On a lightly floured surface, roll the dough out to a $\frac{1}{8}$-inch (3-mm) thickness. Cut the dough into six 6$\frac{1}{2}$-inch-diameter (17-cm) rounds.

Preheat the oven to 425°F (220°C). Divide the fish and shellfish among six 6-inch (15-cm) bowls or individual ramekins. Drizzle some extra-virgin olive oil over. In a small bowl, combine the pine nuts, almonds, garlic, and parsley. Top each ramekin with one fourth of the mixture. Sprinkle with the white wine, lemon juice, salt, and pepper. Top with a basil leaf.

Cover each bowl with a round of pastry dough. Brush the dough with the beaten egg and sprinkle with a few cumin or caraway seeds.

Bake in the preheated oven for 20 minutes, or until the pastry puffs and is golden brown. Remove from the oven and cut around the edge of each pastry lid. Place each upside down on a warmed serving plate. Fill each with the contents of a ramekin and serve immediately.

Makes 6 servings

■ Venetian Tiramisù with Vanilla Sauce ■

Tiramisù alla Veneziana con Salsa alla Vaniglia

The Cipriani's light, not-too-sweet version of this sumptuous Venetian dessert is served in a chocolate shell topped with a gondola-shaped sliver of chocolate. If you don't have time to make the chocolate shells, mold the tiramisù in ramekins. Grate the chocolate and sprinkle it between the mascarpone layers and over the top. Unmold the ramekins to serve.

8 ounces (250 g) bittersweet chocolate, chopped

4 egg yolks

1 cup (4 oz/125 g) powdered sugar, sifted

1 cup (8 oz/250 g) mascarpone cheese* at room temperature

3 egg whites

⅓ cup (3 fl oz/90 ml) cold brewed espresso coffee

Dark rum to taste

12 ladyfingers (savoiardi), halved crosswise (see Basics)

Vanilla Sauce (recipe follows)

On a baking sheet lined with parchment paper, outline 6 gondola shapes (see photo). In a double boiler over barely simmering water, melt the chocolate. Transfer the melted chocolate to a pastry bag and fill in the gondola shapes with the melted chocolate.

Coat the inside of six 3½ inch-diameter, 1-inch-deep paper cases with chocolate. Chill until set. Coat again and chill. Repeat until all the chocolate is used.

Refrigerate the gondolas and paper cases until set, then carefully peel off the parchment paper.

In a medium bowl, beat the egg yolks with ½ cup (2 oz/60 g) of the powdered sugar until pale. Beat in the mascarpone until smooth; do not overbeat, or the mixture may separate.

In a large bowl, beat the egg whites until frothy. Beat in the remaining ½ cup (2 oz/60 g) powdered sugar, a spoonful at a time, until stiff, glossy peaks form. Fold the egg white mixture into the mascarpone mixture.

In a shallow bowl, mix the espresso and rum. Quickly dip the ladyfinger halves on each side and place 2 halves into the bottom of each chocolate shell. Spread a thin layer of mascarpone mixture evenly on top. Add another layer of 2 dipped ladyfinger halves. Using a pastry bag with a large star nozzle or a spoon, add mascarpone mixture to fill each shell. Cover with plastic wrap and refrigerate for at least 4 hours or overnight before serving.

To serve, ladle a pool of vanilla sauce onto each of 6 plates and set a chocolate shell in the center. If you like, spoon a few drops of melted chocolate into the vanilla sauce. Use a skewer to draw a line through the center of each drop to make a decorative wave design (see photo). Dust the chocolate gondolas with cocoa powder and position one on top of each tiramisù.

Makes 6 servings

*Mascarpone, a delicately flavored triple-cream cheese from Lombardy, is usually sold in plastic containers and is available in many grocery stores and most Italian foods stores.

Note: If you are concerned about eating uncooked eggs, do not make this recipe.

Vanilla Sauce

1 cup (8 fl oz/250 ml) milk

½ vanilla bean, split lengthwise, or 1 teaspoon vanilla extract

2 egg yolks

1 tablespoon sugar

½ tablespoon cornstarch

In a small, heavy saucepan, bring the milk and vanilla bean, if using, just to a boil over medium heat. Remove from heat and set aside to infuse for 15 minutes.

In a medium bowl, beat the egg yolks, sugar, and cornstarch together until smooth. Gradually whisk in the milk mixture. Return to the pan and whisk constantly over medium-low heat until the mixture thickens enough to coat a metal spoon. Stir in the vanilla extract, if using. Strain the sauce through a fine-meshed sieve. Set aside and let cool. Cover and refrigerate.

Makes about 1 cup (8 fl oz/250 ml)

FRESCO FROM FIRST CENTURY POMPEII. Still Life with Fish. Museo Archeologico Nazionale, Naples, Italy

DON ALFONSO 1890

Sant'Agata sui Due Golfi, Italy

Located at the tip of the gorgeous Sorrento peninsula between the Bay of Naples and the Bay of Salerno, Don Alfonso is the first restaurant south of Rome to win three stars in the Michelin guide and one of only three in the entire country with three stars in the current edition. Here, you'll enjoy cooking that embodies the warmth and earthiness of a sun-drenched land, with flavors so pure you'll never forget their taste.

Chef Alfonso Iaccarino, grandson of the original Don Alfonso, created gourmet Mediterranean cuisine more than twenty-five years ago, long before Paul Bocuse and other chefs adopted it and made it a worldwide sensation. Chef Iaccarino's exquisite meals taste of the sea and of the organic fruits and vegetables from his family farm, "La Peracciole." The farm, which he tends with his wife Livia, is terraced into a cliff looking across the azure strait of Bocca Piccola to the island of Capri. Their fertile twelve acres produce tomatoes from late spring until mid-January, as well as lemons, olives, eggplants, squash, salad greens, and peppers. Wild oregano, sage, and rosemary grow from cracks in the rocks; native olive and tangerine trees are being reclaimed; and chickens, bees, and cows provide eggs, honey, and milk.

In Don Alfonso's elegant pink-and-green dining room, diners enjoy the fruits of chef Iaccarino's passion for cooking. From the first tastes of spinach, borage, and nettle breads served with a green pool of housemade extra-virgin olive oil, to Iaccarino's signature "crazy water sea bass," to dessert and a thimbleful of homemade limoncello in an elegant stemmed glass, you'll remember Iaccarino's cooking for years. In addition to a seasonal menu, there are two tasting menus, one traditional and one creative. The relaxed, expert service is directed by the beautiful and infinitely charming Livia Iaccarino, and maître d' Constanzo and many of the staff have made service at the restaurant their life's work.

Don Alfonso's celebrated wine cellar, which is carved sixty feet into volcanic rock, was originally an Osci tomb (the Osci lived in this region at the time of the Etruscans, around the sixth and seventh centuries B.C.). The cellar now holds treasures from the finest vineyards of Italy, France, California, and Australia.

There is a small but lovely garden in back of the restaurant, complete with a kiwi tree arbor and seven suites for overnight guests. The Iaccarinos are building new luxury suites, a library, and a space where guests can purchase their outstanding food products and view Alfonso's paintings.

Over such trivialities as these many a valuable hour may slip away, and the traveler who has gone to Italy to study the tactile values of Giotto or the corruption of the Papacy, may return remembering nothing but the blue sky and the men and women who live under it.

—E. M. Forster, *A Room with a View*

DON ALFONSO

MENU

Mozzarella and Cream of Tomato Soufflé
Soufflé di Mozzarella e Crema di Pomodoro

Sea Bass in Crazy Water
Acqua Pazza di Spigola

Linguine with Clams and Zucchini
Linguine alle Vongole Veraci e Zucchine

Candied Ricotta Wrapped in Eggplant and Covered with Chocolate Sauce
Pasticcio di Melanzane con Cioccolata

Mozzarella and Cream of Tomato Soufflé

Soufflé di Mozzarella e Crema di Pomodoro

Olive oil and dried bread crumbs for coating (see Basics)

3 tablespoons butter

¾ cup (4 oz/125 g) all-purpose flour

2 cups (16 fl oz/500 ml) milk

6 eggs, separated

4 fresh basil leaves, finely shredded, plus 4 basil sprigs
   for garnish

¼ teaspoon ground nutmeg

5 ounces (155 g) fresh cow's milk-mozzarella cheese, finely diced

5 Roma (plum) tomatoes seeded, peeled, and puréed (see Basics),
   about 2 cups (16 fl oz/500 ml) purée

Salt and freshly ground pepper to taste

Preheat the oven to 350°F (180°C). Lightly coat four 3-inch (7.5-cm) ramekins with olive oil and dust with bread crumbs, knocking out the excess. In a saucepan over medium heat, melt the butter and stir in the flour; cook, stirring, for 2 minutes. Gradually whisk in the milk and cook, whisking constantly, until smooth and very thick; remove from heat. Stir in the egg yolks, shredded basil, nutmeg, and half the diced mozzarella until smooth and creamy.

In a large bowl, beat the egg whites until stiff, glossy peaks form. Gently fold the egg whites into the mozzarella mixture. Spoon into the prepared ramekins. Place the ramekins in a large baking dish and pour enough hot water into the dish to come halfway up the sides of the ramekins. Bake in the preheated oven for 25 minutes, or until a skewer inserted in the center of a soufflé comes out clean.

In a small saucepan, combine the tomato purée, salt, and pepper. Bring to a simmer and cook for about 30 minutes, or until reduced to the consistency of a thick sauce. To serve, spoon a little tomato sauce in the center of each of 4 plates and sprinkle with the remaining mozzarella cubes. Using a paring knife, loosen the sides of each soufflé and unmold them. Place a soufflé in the center of each of 4 plates, and garnish with a basil sprig.

Makes 4 servings

DON ALFONSO

■ Sea Bass in Crazy Water ■
Acqua Pazza di Spigola

The fanciful name for this dish derives from the "crazy" way the cooking water is transformed into a flavorful broth. Fish in "crazy water" is a classic Neapolitan-style dish, and chef Iaccarino's version is world famous. Years ago a young Japanese chef who trained with him at Don Alfonso returned home to open Acqua Pazza, now an acclaimed restaurant.

4 tablespoons (2 fl oz/60 ml) olive oil

1 onion, thinly sliced

4 Roma (plum) tomatoes, seeded and cut into quarters lengthwise

Salt to taste

½ cup (3 oz/90 g) very finely diced peeled eggplant

½ cup (3 oz/90 g) *each* very finely diced green bell pepper and zucchini

4 fresh basil leaves, minced

4 sea bass or striped bass fillets, quartered

½ cup (4 oz/125 ml) water

4 slices Italian or French bread, lightly toasted

Preheat the oven to 325°F (165°C). In a medium sauté pan or skillet over medium heat, heat 2 tablespoons of the olive oil and sauté the onion for 5 minutes, or until soft and barely golden. Add the tomatoes and salt and cook for about 30 minutes, or until the sauce thickens.

In a large sauté pan or skillet over medium heat, heat the remaining 2 tablespoons olive oil and sauté the eggplant, bell pepper, and zucchini for 10 minutes, or until half cooked. Remove from heat and sprinkle with basil.

In an 8-inch (20-cm) square baking dish, combine the tomato sauce and fish pieces. Cover with the sautéed vegetable mixture and water and season with salt to taste. Cover with aluminum foil and bake in the pre-heated oven for 15 minutes, or until the fish is opaque throughout.

Place a bread crouton in the bottom of each of 4 large soup plates. Top each slice with 4 fish pieces and some of the vegetables. Add a ladle or two of the broth.

Makes 4 servings

■ Linguine with Clams and Zucchini ■
Linguine alle Vongole Veraci e Zucchine

Chef Alfonso Iaccarrino garnishes this flavorful, quickly prepared dish with a thin lengthwise slice of fried zucchini.

5 tablespoons (3 fl oz/80 ml) extra-virgin olive oil

4 zucchini, cut into thin slices

1 shallot, minced

1 garlic clove

2 pounds (1 kg) small clams in their shells, scrubbed

½ cup (⅔ oz/20 g) minced fresh flat-leaf parsley, plus parsley sprigs for garnish

10 ounces (315 g) dried linguine

Preheat the oven to 350°F (180°C). In an 8-inch (20-cm) square baking dish, combine 3 tablespoons of the olive oil and the zucchini. Sprinkle the shallot over. Bake in the preheated oven for 15 minutes.

In a large sauté pan or skillet over medium heat, heat the remaining 2 tablespoons olive oil and sauté the garlic for 2 minutes, or until fragrant; remove the garlic. Add the clams, cover, and cook for 3 to 4 minutes, or until the clams open; discard any unopened clams. Stir in the zucchini minxture and minced parsley. Cook for 2 or 3 minutes; remove from heat.

In a large pot of salted boiling water, cook the linguine for about 9 minutes, or until al dente; drain. Add the linguine to the clams and zucchini and toss over high heat for 1 minute. Tranfer to a large serving bowl or 4 warmed plates, garnish with parsley sprigs, and serve immediately.

Makes 4 servings

DON ALFONSO

■ Candied Ricotta ■ Wrapped in Eggplant and Covered with Chocolate Sauce

Pasticcio di Melanzane con Cioccolata

In this dessert, a dome of ricotta, candied fruit, and chocolate rests on a sponge cake square and is wrapped with thinly sliced eggplant and covered with chocolate sauce. Legend has it that the dish originated in a monastery in Tramonti, located in the mountains above the Amalfi coast town of Maiori. The priory enjoyed eating fried eggplant dipped in a black liqueur until the mid-sixteenth century, when chocolate was introduced to the region. Then they began eating eggplant sweetened with chocolate sauce, now a traditional dish in this region for the Feast of the Assumption on August 15, which is also Ferragosto, the celebration of summer.

⅔ cup (5 oz/155 g) ricotta cheese

⅓ cup (1½ oz/45 g) powdered sugar

⅓ cup (2 oz/60 g) candied fruit, finely diced

8 ounces (250 g) bittersweet chocolate, finely chopped

4 very thin slices eggplant

1 tablespoon sweet Marsala wine,* or to taste

Four 1½-inch (3-cm) sponge cake cubes (see Basics)

In a medium bowl, stir the ricotta and powdered sugar together until well blended. Add the candied fruit and one fourth of the chocolate. Stir until mixed.

Steam the eggplant slices over boiling water in a covered steamer until soft, about 5 minutes; let cool.

In a double boiler over barely simmering water, melt the remaining chocolate and stir in the Marsala.

Place a piece of sponge cake on each of 4 plates and top with a dome of the ricotta mixture. Cover each dome with a slice of eggplant and cover completely with chocolate sauce. Serve immediately.

Makes 4 servings

*Marsala, a rich fortified wine, is available sweet or dry and is produced near the city of Marsala, Sicily.

DON ALFONSO

GIOVANNA GARZONI. A Dish of Broad Beans. Galleria Palatina, Palazzo Pitti, Florence, Italy

GALILEO

Washington, D.C.

Galileo is the flagship restaurant of the superbly gifted chef Roberto Donna. "Galileo will always by my showcase, offering the best of Piedmontese cuisine. It is very close to my heart," Donna says. Born in San Raffaele Cimena, a hamlet of about 400 people in Italy's Piedmont region, he has been passionate about cooking since grade school. Watching chefs in the restaurant kitchen next to his parent's grocery store was a favorite childhood pastime, and by age nine Donna had his own chef's knife and was helping with the cooking. He enrolled in a professional cooking school at thirteen and graduated with highest honor. Arriving in Washington, D.C. at the age of nineteen with a suitcase full of pots and pans and a job offer as sous-chef at Romeo and Juliet, Donna became head chef within eighteen months. In 1984, he opened Galileo, where he introduced the cuisine of his native Piedmont to Washington, D.C. During the past sixteen years, he has worked hard to educate consumers about authentic Italian food and wine and to preserve the legacy of Italian roots and traditions for future generations. Today, Washington has as many fine Italian restaurants as French ones, and over the years some of the best chefs in these kitchens have cooked at Galileo.

Donna's success at Galileo has led him to open twelve other establishments in the Washington area, and his work has received worldwide praise. He is a former chairman of the Gruppo Ristorantore Italiani, an international organization devoted to maintaining the traditions and standards of classical Italian cooking, and was awarded the Insegna del Ristorante Italiano by the Italian president, who named Galileo one of the world's twenty finest Italian restaurants.

Donna's menus are composed daily, and three days a week a fixed-price tasting menu is offered in Il Laboratorio del Galileo, a state-of-the-art kitchen and private dining area adjacent to the main dining room. Here, the chef entertains and creates a fabulous ten- to twelve-course tasting menu for about thirty guests. Galileo's extensive wine cellar of vintages from Italy, France, and the United States was awarded *Wine Spectator* magazine's 1999 Grand Award of Excellence. The following recipes were presented to Menus and Music by chef Roberto Donna.

MENU

Lettuce Leaves Stuffed with Ricotta and Vegetables
with a Fava Bean Sauce

Lattughe Ripiene di Ricotta e Vegetali in Salsa di Fave

Zucchini and Shrimp Ravioli

Ravioli di Zucchine e Gamberi

Roasted Rack of Veal with Pancetta, Jerusalem Artichokes,
Black Truffles, and Spinach

Costolette di Vitello con Pancetta, Topinambur,
Tartufo Nero, e Spinaci

Grandmother Rita's Molded Chocolate Pudding

Bunet della Nonna Rita

Lettuce Leaves Stuffed with Ricotta and Vegetables with a Fava Bean Sauce

Lattughe Ripiene di Ricotta e Vegetali in Salsa di Fave

Giardiniera

2 tablespoons olive oil

2 garlic cloves

⅔ cup (3 oz/90 g) finely diced zucchini

⅔ cup (3 oz/90 g) finely diced celery

⅓ cup (1½ oz/45 g) *each* finely diced red and yellow bell pepper

⅔ cup (3 oz/90 g) finely diced peeled eggplant

⅔ cup (3 oz/90 g) finely diced onion

Salt and freshly ground pepper to taste

8 Boston or butter lettuce leaves

1 cup (8 oz/250 g) ricotta cheese

5 ounces (155 g) mozzarella cheese, finely diced (about 1 cup)

¾ cup (3 oz/90 g) freshly grated Parmesan cheese

1 cup (5 oz/155 g) shelled fava beans

4 tablespoons (2 oz/160 g) butter, cut into small pieces

6 tablespoons (3 fl oz/80 ml) olive oil

3 shallots, minced

2 tablespoons minced fresh basil leaves

To make the giardiniera: In a large skillet or sauté pan over medium heat, heat the olive oil and sauté the garlic and vegetables for 2 minutes. Remove the garlic cloves and season the vegetables with salt and pepper. Remove from heat and transfer the vegetables to a colander; drain and let cool.

In a large pot of salted boiling water, blanch 1 lettuce leaf for 5 seconds. Using a slotted spoon, transfer the leaf to paper towels and spread it out flat to dry. Repeat with the remaining lettuce leaves.

Preheat the oven to 350°F (180°C). In a medium bowl, stir together the ricotta, giardiniera, mozzarella, and Parmesan until well blended.

Cook the fava beans in salted boiling water for 3 minutes. Drain and rinse under cold water. Using your fingernail, tear off a small piece of skin from the rounded end of each bean; squirt out the bean by pinching the opposite end. Chop the beans and set aside.

Place 1 tablespoon of the ricotta mixture in the center of each blanched lettuce leaf. Fold up the bottom and the sides, then fold down the top to form 8 purses. Place the purses in an 8-inch (20-cm) square baking dish. Add the butter, olive oil, shallots, and fava beans. Bake in the preheated oven for 10 minutes.

Remove from the oven and transfer the purses to a plate. Stir the basil into the fava bean mixture. Arrange a bed of the fava bean mixture on each of 4 warmed plates. Top each with 2 lettuce leaf purses and serve very hot.

Makes 4 servings

▪ Zucchini and Shrimp Ravioli ▪
Ravioli di Zucchine e Gamberi

Pasta

1½ cups (7½ oz/235 g) all-purpose flour

4 eggs

Filling

1 pound (500 g) zucchini (about 3 zucchini), coarsely chopped

⅔ cup (5 oz/155 g) ricotta cheese

¼ teaspoon minced fresh marjoram

Salt and freshly ground pepper to taste

Sauce

3 tablespoons olive oil

2 garlic cloves

1 shallot

10 ounces (315 g) tomatoes, peeled, seeded, and coarsely chopped
  (see Basics)

1 pound cooked shrimp

Grated zest of 1 small orange

Pinch of minced fresh flat-leaf parsley

Minced fresh marjoram to taste

Salt and freshly ground pepper to taste

To make the pasta: Pour the flour into a mound on a work surface and make a well in the center. Add the eggs to the well and beat lightly with a fork just until blended. Begin mixing the flour into the eggs, drawing the flour from the inside wall of the well, until a dough is formed. Alternatively, combine the ingredients in a food processor and process just until a ball is formed. On a floured work surface, knead the dough until smooth and elastic, about 8 minutes. Divide the dough into 4 equal portions, enclose each with plastic wrap, and let rest for 2 hours.

Cook the zucchini in salted boiling water for 15 minutes, or until tender when pierced with a knife; drain. Transfer the zucchini to a blender or food processor. Add the ricotta, marjoram, salt, and pepper and purée.

Set the rollers of a pasta machine at the highest number. (The rollers will be wide apart.) Flatten one piece of dough into a rough rectangle. Feed the rectangle of pasta through the rollers. Fold in half and feed through the rollers 8 or 9 more times, folding the dough in half each time and dusting with flour, if necessary, to prevent sticking. Turn the dial down one notch and feed the dough through the rollers without folding. Continue to feed the dough through the rollers without folding, turning the dial one notch lower each time until the second-lowest notch is reached. The dough will be a smooth long sheet, 4 to 5 inches (10 to 13 cm) wide and about $\frac{1}{16}$ inch (2 mm) thick.

On one half of the dough place teaspoonfuls of the filling in a row, about 2 inches (5 cm) apart. Brush around each mound with water. Fold over the other half of the dough and press firmly to seal. Using a fluted pasta wheel or knife, cut the pasta to make ravioli of the desired size and shape; make certain the edges are sealed. Sprinkle the ravioli with flour and refrigerate until ready to cook.

To make the sauce: In a large skillet or sauté pan over medium heat, heat the olive oil and sauté the garlic and shallot for 3 minutes, or until barely golden. Using a slotted spoon, remove the garlic and shallot. Add the tomatoes and shrimp and cook for 2 minutes. Stir in the orange zest and remove from heat. Stir in the parsley, marjoram, salt, and pepper.

Cook the ravioli in a large pot of salted boiling water until they float to the top, about 3 minutes. Gently drain the ravioli and transfer to a warmed serving bowl. Gently toss with the tomato sauce and serve immediately.

Makes 4 servings

■ Roasted Rack of Veal ■
with Pancetta, Jerusalem Artichokes, Black Truffles, and Spinach

Costolette di Vitello con Pancetta, Topinambur,
Tartufo Nero, e Spinaci

One 2-pound (1-kg) rack of veal, or 4 veal loin chops

Salt and freshly ground pepper to taste

½ cup (4 fl oz/125 ml) water

1 cup (8 fl oz/250 ml) homemade beef broth or chicken broth (see Basics) or canned low-salt chicken broth, plus more as needed for spinach purée

20 coffee beans, lightly crushed with a pan

Grated zest of 1 lemon

1 cup (8 fl oz/250 ml) milk

1 pound (500 g) Jerusalem artichokes*, peeled and finely diced

1 cup (8 fl oz/250 ml) heavy (whipping) cream

1 ounce (30 g) black truffles, minced

3 ounces (90 g) thinly sliced pancetta, cut into fine strips

¼ cup (2 fl oz/60 ml) olive oil

6 ounces (185 g) baby spinach

1 garlic clove

Preheat the oven to 400°F (200°C). Cut the rack in half. Season with salt and pepper and place on a baking pan. Bake, turning occasionally, in the preheated oven for 12 minutes. Remove from the oven and transfer the veal to a plate. Stir the water, 1 cup (8 fl oz/250 ml) broth, and coffee beans into the pan. Set aside for 10 minutes. Strain the sauce through a fine-meshed sieve. Stir in the lemon zest.

In a medium saucepan, combine the milk and Jerusalem artichokes and cook over medium-high heat until crisp-tender, about 7 minutes. Drain and set the Jerusalem artichokes aside. In a medium saucepan, cook the cream over medium-high heat to reduce by half. Add the

Jerusalem artichokes and truffles.

In a small sauté pan or skillet, sauté the pancetta until the fat has rendered. Using a slotted spoon, transfer to paper towels, then add to the sauce.

In a sauté pan or skillet over medium heat, heat the olive oil and sauté the spinach with the garlic until just wilted. Remove the garlic and transfer the spinach to a blender or food processor and purée; if the purée is too thick, add a little chicken broth.

Cut the veal into thin slices. Serve with a spoonful of the artichoke mixture and the sauce. Decorate with spinach purée and serve immediately.

Makes 4 servings

*Jerusalem artichokes, members of the sunflower family, are knobby potatolike tubers native to North America. First cultivated in Europe in Rome around 1617, their taste resembles that of an artichoke.

■ Grandmother Rita's ■
Molded Chocolate Pudding

Bunet della Nonna Rita

Caramel syrup coats this baked chocolate pudding flavored with Fernet-Branca or rum.

6 eggs

6 tablespoons (3 oz/90 g) sugar

40 amaretti cookies, about 8 ounces (250 g) total, chopped

3 tablespoons unsweetened cocoa powder

1 tablespoon grated sweet chocolate

¼ cup (2 fl oz/60 ml) Fernet-Branca* or rum

2 cups (16 fl oz/500 ml) milk, warmed

Caramel

⅓ cup (3 oz/90 g) sugar

3 tablespoons water

Preheat the oven to 350°F (180°C). Combine the eggs and 6 tablespoons (3 oz/90 g) sugar in a medium bowl. Using an electric mixer, beat the eggs and sugar for 5 minutes, or until pale in color and a slowly dissolving ribbon forms on the surface when a beater is lifted. Add the cookies, cocoa powder, grated chocolate, and Fernet or rum and blend. Add the milk and mix again; set aside.

To make the caramel: In a small, heavy pan, combine sugar and water. Bring to a boil over high heat and cook until golden brown. Immediately remove the caramel from heat and pour into the bottom of an 8-by-4-inch (20-by-10-cm) loaf pan.

Pour in the chocolate mixture and place the loaf pan in a baking pan. Add water to the baking pan to reach halfway up the sides of the loaf pan. Bake in the preheated oven for 45 minutes, or until a knife inserted in the center of the pudding comes out clean. Remove from the oven and let cool completely. To serve, invert the pan onto a serving platter. The caramel will coat the dessert.

*Fernet-Branca is a very strong-tasting, bitter herbal digestivo (a drink taken after dinner to aid the digestion).

GENOA

Portland, Oregon

Stepping through the front door of Genoa restaurant, customers are at once surrounded by warm light, gorgeous flowers, and enticing aromas. Known for its delicious seven-course fixed-price dinners, Genoa has been highly regarded by diners and critics alike for over thirty years and was named Portland's favorite restaurant by the Zagat Survey.

The restaurant's small square dining room holds ten tables, and the menu, which changes every two to three weeks, takes diners on a leisurely tour of Northern Italian cuisine. Less elaborate four-course meals are available Monday through Thursday. Part-owner and executive chef Catherine Whims works with her sous-chefs to research and orchestrate the menus. The sequence of dishes, from seasonal antipasti to a dazzling dessert tray, always showcases Portland's bounty of excellent local ingredients, which include wild mushrooms, tender greens, game, and luscious fruits. Some ingredients are even Italian transports, such as the chard grown from seeds brought from Italy by a member of the Genoa staff. The meals are overseen by part-owner Kerry DeBuse, the restaurant's gracious headwaiter. Genoa's extensive and carefully selected wine list offers Italian, French, California, and Northwest wines. The following menu and recipes were created by chef Catherine Whims for Menus and Music.

GIUSEPPE ARCIMBOLDO. Vertumnus (Emperor Rudolf II). Slott, Skokloster, Sweden

MENU

Crostini with Chicken Livers
Crostini di Fegatini

Pumpkin Cappellacci
Cappellacci con la Zucca alla Ferrarese

Roasted Fillet of Beef with an Alba-Style White Truffle Sauce
Arrosto di Bue all'Albese

Sautéed Greens
Verdura Saltati

Espresso Coffee Gelato
Gelato al Caffè

Human beings in the world we are the same
As coffee-beans before the espresso machine:
First one, and then another, a steady stream,
All of 'em going alike to one sure fate.
—Giuseppe Gioacchino Belli,
from "The Coffee House Philosopher"

▪ Crostini with Chicken Livers ▪
Crostini di Fegatini

A classic Tuscan antipasto.

2 tablespoons butter

1 tablespoon olive oil

¼ cup (1 oz/30 g) minced onion

2 bay leaves

8 ounces (250 g) chicken livers, trimmed, rinsed, and patted dry

¼ cup dry Marsala wine

2 anchovy fillets

2 teaspoons capers

Salt and freshly ground pepper to taste

12 crostini (see Basics)

Minced fresh flat-leaf parsley for garnish

In a large sauté pan or skillet over medium heat, melt the butter with the olive oil and sauté the onion for 3 minutes, or until soft. Add the bay leaves and chicken livers and sauté for 8 to 10 minutes, or until the livers are browned on the outside but still pink on the inside. Using a slotted spoon, transfer the livers to a chopping board.

Pour in the Marsala and stir to scrape up any browned bits on the bottom of the pan. Boil until the Marsala has almost evaporated; remove the bay leaves. Finely chop the livers with the anchovies and capers. Return the liver mixture to the pan over high heat, season with salt and pepper, and sauté for 1 minute. Spoon the liver on the toasts, garnish with parsley, and serve.

Makes 6 servings

■ Pumpkin Cappellacci ■

Cappellacci con la Zucca alla Ferrarese

Literally "shabby old hats," cappellacci are stuffed pasta triangles formed into ring shapes that resemble pointed hats.

Green Butter

½ cup (4 oz/125 g) unsalted butter at room temperature

1½ tablespoons minced fresh flat-leaf parsley

1 teaspoon minced fresh marjoram

1 tablespoon minced fresh sage

1 garlic clove, minced

¼ teaspoon salt

Filling

1 small sugar pumpkin, halved and seeded, or piece of butternut squash, about 3 pounds (1.5 kg)

1 small sweet potato, halved

⅓ cup (1½ oz/45 g) grated Parmesan cheese

½ cup (2 oz/60 g) crushed amaretti cookies

1 egg yolk

2 tablespoons unsalted butter, melted

Pinch of grated nutmeg

Salt and freshly ground pepper to taste

Pasta Dough

2 cups (10 oz/315 g) all-purpose flour, plus more if needed

2 eggs

2 to 3 tablespoons heavy (whipping) cream

1 teaspoon salt

Freshly grated Parmesan cheese for tossing and serving

Coarsely ground pepper to taste

To make the green butter: In a medium bowl, combine all the ingredients and stir until blended. Set aside at room temperature to use now, or cover and refrigerate for up to 3 days. Bring to room temperature before using.

To make the filling: Preheat the oven to 375°F (190°C). Brush a baking sheet with olive oil and place the pumpkin or squash and sweet potato, cut-sides down, on the prepared pan. Bake in the preheated oven about for 45 minutes, or until soft when pierced with a knife. Turn cut-sides up and bake 10 minutes longer; let cool. Scoop out the flesh and transfer it to a medium bowl. Mash with a potato masher. Add the remaining ingredients. Stir until blended. Cover and refrigerate for 30 minutes, or until chilled.

To make the pasta: Pour the flour into a mound on a work surface and make a well in the center. Add the eggs, cream, and salt to the well. Using a fork, beat the eggs and cream lightly and gradually mix the flour into the egg mixture until a dough is formed. Add more flour, if the dough is sticky. Alternatively, combine the flour, eggs, cream, and salt in a food processor and process until the mixture just forms a ball.

On a floured work surface, knead the dough for about 8 minutes, or until smooth. Cut the dough into 4 equal sections, cover with plastic wrap, and let rest for 1 hour.

Set the rollers of a pasta machine at the highest number. Flatten one piece of dough into a rough rectangle. Feed the rectangle of pasta through the rollers. Fold in half and feed through the rollers 8 or 9 more times, folding the dough in half each time. Turn the dial down one notch and feed the dough through the rollers without folding. Continue to feed the dough through the rollers without folding, turning the dial one notch lower each time until the second-lowest notch is reached. The dough will be a long, smooth sheet 4 to 5 inches (10 cm to 13 cm) wide.

On one half of the dough, place teaspoonfuls of the filling about 1½ inches apart in a row. Brush around the filling with water. Fold over the other half of the dough and press firmly between the mounds of filling to seal. Using a fluted pasta wheel or a knife, cut the pasta to make ravioli; make certain the edges are sealed. After dipping your fingers in water, press two opposing corners of the ravioli together to form cappellacci. Repeat to roll and fill the remaining dough, 1 piece at a time.

Put the green butter in a large warmed pasta bowl. Drop the cappellacci into a large pot of salted boiling water and cover the pot. Remove the lid as soon as the water returns to a boil. As soon as the cappellacci float to the surface, drain gently and transfer to the bowl with the butter. Gently toss and sprinkle with Parmesan cheese and coarsely ground pepper. Serve immediately, with a bowl of grated Parmesan cheese on the side.

Makes 8 to 10 servings

◼ Roasted Fillet of Beef ◼
with an Alba-Style White Truffle Sauce
Arrosto di Bue all'Albese

A special dish for an autumn or winter dinner party, when Italian white truffles are in season. Tartufo bianco d'Alba, found in the area south of Alba in Piedmont, have been called "the diamonds of the table" and are greatly prized in Italian cooking. The richly flavored truffle sauce may be prepared ahead and reheated just before serving.

Truffle Sauce

1 tablespoon butter

1 tablespoon flour

1 cup (8 fl oz/250 ml) reduced beef broth (see Basics)

2 small white truffles, grated (see Resources)

4 anchovy fillets

1 shallot, minced

1 garlic clove, minced

¼ cup (⅓ oz/10 g) minced fresh flat-leaf parsley

1 hard-cooked egg yolk

Fresh lemon juice, extra-virgin olive oil, and freshly ground pepper to taste

2 tablespoons olive oil

One 2½-pound (1.25-kg) beef tenderloin

2 small white truffles, shaved (see Resources), or white truffle oil* for drizzling

Preheat the oven to 475°F (245°C). To make the truffle sauce: In a small saucepan, bring the beef broth to a simmer over medium-low heat.

In a small saucepan, melt the butter over medium heat and stir in the flour; stir constantly for 2 or 3 minutes. Whisk in the broth until the sauce is smooth. Reduce heat to low, and simmer, stirring frequently.

Using a mortar and pestle, pound the truffles, anchovies, shallot, garlic, parsley, and egg yolk to a paste. Press the paste through a fine-meshed sieve into the simmering sauce and continue to simmer for 3 to 5 minutes to blend the flavors. Season the sauce with lemon juice, olive oil, and pepper. Set aside and keep warm.

In a large skillet or sauté pan over high heat, heat the olive oil and quickly brown the fillet on all sides. Transfer the meat to a roasting pan with a rack and roast in the preheated oven until medium rare, about 10 minutes. Remove from the oven and let rest for 5 minutes.

Slice the beef into ½-inch-thick (12-mm) slices. Spoon a little of the truffle sauce onto each of 6 plates, fan a few slices of beef on top, and garnish with shaved truffles or a drizzle of truffle oil. Serve immediately.

Makes 6 servings

*White truffle oil is available in specialty foods stores and Italian markets (also see Resources).

■ Sautéed Greens ■
Verdura Saltati

Sautéed escarole, spinach, and broccoli rabe are an excellent accompaniment to any hearty meat dish.

¼ cup (2 fl oz/60 ml) olive oil

2 garlic cloves, minced

¼ teaspoon red pepper flakes

Leaves from 1 large head escarole, chopped, or 2 bunches spinach
 or 1 bunch broccoli rabe, stemmed and chopped

Salt and freshly ground pepper to taste

In a large, heavy saucepan over medium heat, heat the olive oil and sauté the garlic and red pepper flakes for 2 minutes, or until the garlic is barely golden. Raise heat to high, add the escarole, spinach, or broccoli rabe, and toss until the greens are wilted and tender, about 5 minutes. Season with salt and pepper; drain, but do not squeeze. Serve hot.

Makes 6 servings

■ Espresso Coffee Gelato ■
Gelato al Caffè

One of Italy's great culinary creations, gelato is an all-time favorite dessert. This not-too-sweet version is a perfect finale for any dinner party.

3 cups (24 fl oz/750 ml) heavy (whipping) cream

½ cup (1 oz/30 g) Italian-roast coffee beans

⅓ cup (3 fl oz/80 ml) brewed espresso

4 egg yolks

⅓ cup (2½ oz/75 g) sugar

In a double boiler over simmering water, combine 2 cups (16 fl oz/500 ml) of the cream, the coffee beans, and espresso. Cook, stirring occasionally, until bubbles form around the edges and the cream tastes strongly of coffee, at least 30 minutes.

In a large bowl, whisk the egg yolks just until blended. In a thin stream, gradually whisk the hot cream mixture into the yolks. Place the bowl over a pan of barely simmering water and cook, whisking constantly, until the mixture thickens enough to coat the back of a spoon. Remove from heat, stir in the sugar, and set the bowl in a slightly larger bowl filled with crushed ice; whisk until cool. Cover the bowl with plastic wrap and refrigerate the custard until cold, at least 2 hours. Pour the mixture through a fine-meshed sieve and stir in the remaining 1 cup (8 fl oz/250 ml) cream. Freeze in an ice cream maker according to the manufacturer's instructions.

Makes about 2 pints

MI PIACI

Dallas, Texas

Italian cuisine is very popular in the Dallas/Fort Worth area, and Mi Piaci (which means "you are pleasing to me" in Italian) is one of the most popular of the region's restaurants. According to Gourmet magazine, it ranks as one of the top twenty restaurants in Dallas, while D magazine ranks it in the top twenty-five. Floor-to-ceiling windows overlooking a beautiful pond, and thirty-five-foot-high twisting white columns create a visually stunning room that has won architectural awards and is an appropriate backdrop for the wonderful food found here.

Executive chef Kevin Ascolese's menu evokes the Italian countryside with Tuscan influences. His dishes include housemade sausages, grilled vegetables, and outstanding fresh pastas, and some of the fresh herbs he uses in the kitchen are grown on the restaurant's rooftop! Ascolese is a firm believer in keeping things simple in the kitchen. He updates classic Italian recipes with new twists, giving each dish its own personality. Owners Phil and Janet Cobb spend time every year in Italy researching trends, discovering resources, and studying Italian food history. Mi Piaci has a user-friendly wine list, with all wines grouped according to style and briefly described. More than two hundred Italian wines are available, from readily drinkable recent vintages to truly great noble reds, and in 1996, Mi Piaci was given an Award of Excellence by *Wine Spectator* magazine. The following menu and recipes were presented to Menus and Music by chef Kevin Ascolese.

MENU

Field Greens with Balsamic Vinaigrette

Insalata di Tricolore con Balsamico

Risotto with Porcini Mushrooms and Asparagus

Risotto con Porcini e Asparagi

Red Snapper with Grilled Tomatoes and Fresh Spinach

Pesce con Pomodoro e Spinaci

Burned Espresso Cream

Crema di Espresso

▪ Field Greens ▪
with Balsamic Vinaigrette
Insalata di Tricolore con Balsamico

2 tablespoons pine nuts

2 ounces (60 g) pancetta, chopped

8 large handfuls mixed salad greens

Balsamic Vinaigrette (recipe follows)

4 ounces (125 g) Gorgonzola, crumbled (4/5 cup)

3 Roma (plum) tomatoes, seeded and sliced lengthwise into quarters

Salt and freshly ground pepper to taste

In a dry sauté pan or skillet over medium heat, toss the pine nuts until pale golden; do not let them brown. Empty into a bowl and set aside.

In a sauté pan or skillet over medium-low heat, sauté the pancetta until the fat is rendered. Increase heat to medium and fry until the pancetta is crisp. Using a slotted spoon, transfer to paper towels to drain.

In a medium bowl, combine the greens and balsamic vinaigrette and toss very well. Arrange a mound of salad on each of 4 plates and sprinkle with the pine nuts, Gorgonzola, and pancetta. Surround each salad with 3 tomato slices. Sprinkle the tomatoes with salt and pepper.

Makes 4 servings

Balsamic Vinaigrette

6 tablespoons (3 fl oz/80 ml) extra-virgin olive oil

2 tablespoons balsamic vinegar

1 tablespoon minced fresh oregano

1 tablespoon chopped fresh basil

1 tablespoon minced shallot

1 teaspoon minced garlic cloves

Salt and freshly ground pepper to taste

In a small bowl, whisk all the ingredients together.

Makes about ¹⁄₂ cup (4 fl oz/125 ml)

■ Risotto with Porcini Mushrooms ■ and Asparagus

Risotto con Porcini e Asparagi

A drizzle of white truffle oil gives this risotto an extra dimension, but it is delicious without any garnish at all.

2 ounces (60 g) dried porcini mushrooms

1 small bunch asparagus (about 20 spears), trimmed and cut into 2-inch (5-cm) pieces

6 cups (48 fl oz/1.5 l) chicken broth (see Basics) or canned low-salt chicken broth

2 tablespoons olive oil

1 small onion, minced

1½ cups (10 oz/285 g) Arborio rice

Salt and freshly ground pepper to taste

White truffle oil for drizzling

In a small bowl, soak the porcini in hot water to cover for 30 minutes. Drain the porcini, reserving the soaking liquid.

In a large pot of salted boiling water, blanch the asparagus for 2 minutes. Drain and immerse in ice water to stop the cooking; drain again and set aside.

In a large saucepan, bring the broth to a simmer. In a medium, heavy saucepan over medium heat, heat the olive oil and sauté the onion until soft, about 3 minutes. Add the rice and stir to coat well with the oil, about 2 minutes. Add ½ cup of the broth and stir constantly until absorbed. Repeat until all the broth has been used. Add the porcini and all but the last ½ inch (12 mm) of the reserved mushroom liquid. Cook, stirring constantly, until the liquid is absorbed. The rice should be al dente, tender but firm. Stir in the asparagus, salt, and pepper. Serve at once in warmed shallow bowls, drizzled with the truffle oil.

Makes 4 servings

▪ Red Snapper ▪
with Grilled Tomatoes and Fresh Spinach

Pesce con Pomodoro e Spinaci

1 yellow or red tomato, cut into 8 slices

1 Roma (plum) tomato, cut lengthwise into 8 slices

Salt and freshly ground pepper to taste

4 handfuls baby spinach leaves, or 1 bunch spinach, stemmed

12 Belgian endive leaves

2 tablespoons olive oil

4 red snapper fillets

¼ cup (2 fl oz/60 ml) Mustard-Shallot Vinaigrette (recipe follows)

2 tablespoons chopped fresh chives for garnish

Preheat the broiler. Sprinkle the tomato slices with salt and pepper. Place on a broiler pan lined with aluminum foil and broil 2 inches (5 cm) from the heat source until lightly browned.

Arrange 4 tomato slices on each of 4 plates. Top each serving with a small mound of spinach and 3 endive leaves.

In a large skillet or sauté pan over medium-high heat, heat the olive oil. Season the fish with salt and pepper to taste and place in the pan, skin-side down. Sauté the fish until browned, about 3 minutes on each side. Arrange a fish fillet on top of each mound of spinach. Drizzle the vinaigrette over. Sprinkle with chives and serve immediately.

Makes 4 servings

Mustard-Shallot Vinaigrette

2 teaspoons Dijon mustard

1 tablespoon minced shallots

2 tablespoons fresh lemon juice

6 tablespoons (3 fl oz/80 ml) extra virgin olive oil

In a small bowl, whisk all the ingredients together.

Makes about 1 cup (8 fl oz/250 ml)

■ Burned Espresso Cream ■
Crema di Espresso

2 cups (16 fl oz/500 ml) heavy (whipping) cream

1 cup (8 fl oz/250 ml) whole milk

½ vanilla bean, split lengthwise, or 1 teaspoon vanilla extract

¼ cup (1½ oz/45 g) finely ground espresso

½ cup (4 oz/120 g) sugar

3 large eggs

4 tablespoons (1½ oz/45 g) packed brown sugar

4 fresh raspberries

4 fresh strawberries, hulled and sliced

4 fresh blackberries

4 fresh mint sprigs

4 biscotti (see Basics)

Preheat the oven to 250°F (120°C). In a small, heavy saucepan, combine the cream, milk, vanilla bean, if using, and espresso and cook over medium heat until bubbles form around the edges of the pan. Remove from heat, cover, and set aside to steep for 15 minutes.

In a medium stainless-steel bowl, whisk the sugar and eggs together until blended. Place over a saucepan of simmering water and whisk constantly until very thick. Gradually whisk in the cream mixture. Remove from heat and set aside to cool for 1½ hours, whisking every 15 minutes. Remove the vanilla bean, if using. Stir in the vanilla extract, if using. Pour into 4 individual ramekins and refrigerate for 4 to 6 hours.

Just before serving, preheat the broiler. Place 1 tablespoon of the brown sugar in a small fine-meshed sieve and push the sugar through with the back of a spoon to evenly layer the top of a custard. Repeat with the remaining custards. Place the custards on a baking sheet about 2 inches from the heat source and broil until the sugar is melted and crisp, about 1 minute; be careful not to burn. Let the custards cool for a few minutes.

In a small bowl, combine the raspberries, strawberries, and blackberries. Spoon the berry mixture over the custards and garnish with mint. Serve with biscotti.

Makes 4 servings

REMI

New York, New York

Remi combines the rich tradition of Venetian cuisine with the romance and elegance of Venetian design and architecture, in an innovative, contemporary style.

Francesco Antonucci, Venetian-born chef and co-proprietor, dazzles diners with his inspired interpretations of classic Venetian dishes: mouthwatering antipasti, homemade pastas and risottos, sensational fish dishes, and tempting desserts. Antonucci is the author of *Venetian Taste* and *The Art of Regional Italian Cooking*. Co-proprietor Adam D. Tihany, one of the world's preeminent restaurant designers, has created a dining atmosphere that is at once festive and sophisticated. As a result, dining at Remi is like embarking on a luxury cruise through Venice. (*Remi* means "oars" in Italian.) An expansive fantasy mural of a grand canal by Paris Paulin is the highlight of the soaring main dining room, with its flying buttress archways, nautical blue-and-white-striped banquettes, and stunning Venetian glass chandeliers that complement the bar's fine collection of contemporary and antique Venetian glasses. Remi offers three other elegant dining spaces: the Atrium Garden, a seasonally opened glass-roofed garden; the Rialto Room, a private dining room for up to 125 people; and the Chef's Table, a private dining room off the kitchen for up to fourteen people. The following menu and recipes were created by chef Francesco Antonucci.

JACOPO LIGOZZI. Sea Bream. Gabinetto dei Disegni e delle Stampe, Florence, Italy

MENU

Octopus Salad with Marinated Radicchio
Polipo con Radicchio

Tuna Ravioli with Ginger, Marco Polo Style
Ravioli "Marco Polo" con Tonno e Zenzero

Halibut with Broccoli
Filetti di Pesce con Broccoli

Apple-Mascarpone Tart
Torta di Mele e Mascarpone

■ Octopus Salad ■ with Marinated Radicchio

Polipo con Radicchio

Combining marinated radicchio with octopus results in a handsome dish with a rich purple color. The succulence and mild sweetness of the octopus complements the tangy and delicately bitter flavor of the radicchio. When cooking the octopus, Francesco throws a few used wine corks into the pot, a technique that is supposed to keep the octopus tender. Putting the octopus in cold water after it is boiled helps to set the color.

1 pound (500 g) baby octopus, cleaned

1 cup (8 fl oz/250 ml) white vinegar

1 tablespoon black peppercorns

2 celery stalks, coarsely chopped

1 onion, quartered

5 cups (40 fl oz/1.25 l) water

3 tablespoons extra-virgin olive oil

1½ teaspoons red wine vinegar

Salt and freshly ground pepper to taste

1 tablespoon chopped fresh flat-leaf parsley

Marinated Radicchio, drained (recipe follows)

In a large saucepan, combine the octopus, vinegar, peppercorns, celery, onion, and water. The water should cover the octopus. Add 2 or 3 used wine corks. Bring to a boil, reduce heat, and simmer for 1 hour. Drain the octopus and transfer to a bowl of ice water; let cool completely.

Cut the octopus tentacles into 1-inch (2.5-cm) pieces. (Throw the heads away.) In a medium bowl, mix the olive oil, red wine vinegar, salt, pepper, and parsley together and toss with the octopus. Set aside and let marinate at least 1 hour.

Arrange the octopus on each of 4 plates, with marinated radicchio on the side.

Makes 4 servings

Marinated Radicchio

Francesco learned this recipe from his friends at Ristorante Celeste in Treviso. Marinating radicchio removes some of its bitterness and intensifies its color.

2½ cups (20 fl oz/625 ml) water

1 cup (8 fl oz/250 ml) white wine vinegar

2 tablespoons sugar

1½ teaspoons salt

1½ teaspoon black peppercorns

¾ teaspoon juniper berries, crushed

4 heads radicchio

1 cup (8 fl oz/250 ml) extra-virgin olive oil

¼ bunch fresh flat-leaf parsley sprigs

In a large saucepan, combine the water, vinegar, sugar, salt, 1 teaspoon of the peppercorns, and ½ teaspoon of the juniper berries. Bring to a boil.

If using round heads of radicchio, quarter them. Treviso radicchio, with elongated leaves, may be halved. Place the radicchio in the saucepan and cook for 6 to 7 minutes; remove from heat and drain well.

Transfer the radicchio to a bowl or large jar and cover with the olive oil. Add the remaining ½ teaspoon peppercorns and ¼ teaspoon juniper berries and tuck in the parsley. Cover and marinate for 4 to 5 hours, or refrigerate for up to 1 week.

Makes 8 servings

▪ Tuna Ravioli ▪
with Ginger, Marco Polo Style
Ravioli "Marco Polo" con Tonno e Zenzero

Created by Francesco Antonucci and inspired by Adam Tihany, this is Remi's signature dish. Ravioli filled with fresh tuna is spiced with fresh ginger. Although the Romans had ginger, its cultivation eventually disappeared. The Venetian Marco Polo reintroduced it to Europe in the thirteenth century. These intriguingly spicy ravioli are served in a light tomato sauce with fried ginger on top. Sheets of commercial fresh pasta may be substituted for homemade.

1 tablespoon extra-virgin olive oil

2 tablespoons finely diced carrot

2 tablespoons finely diced onion

2 tablespoons finely diced fennel

1 teaspoon minced fresh ginger, plus one 2-inch (5-cm) piece peeled fresh ginger, sliced paper thin and cut into thin strips

12 ounces (375 g) tuna fillets, finely chopped

¼ cup (2 oz/60 g) ricotta cheese, drained for at least 4 hours

Salt and freshly ground pepper to taste

1¼ pounds (625 g) fresh pasta, or 6 sheets commercial fresh pasta

1 large egg yolk beaten with 2 tablespoons water

Flour for dusting

2 tablespoons canola oil

4 tablespoons (2 oz/60 g) unsalted butter

1⅓ cups (8 oz/250 g) chopped fresh or well-drained canned tomatoes

¼ cup (2 fl oz/60 ml) fish stock (see Basics) or canned low-salt chicken broth

1 teaspoon minced fresh tarragon

In a medium, heavy sauté pan or skillet over medium heat, heat the olive oil and sauté the carrot, onion, fennel, and minced ginger for about 5 minutes, or until the vegetables are tender. Remove from heat and let cool briefly. Mix in the tuna and ricotta. Season with salt and pepper.

Spread 3 sheets of pasta on a lightly floured work surface. Place slightly rounded tablespoonfuls of the filling in rows 2 inches (5 cm) apart on the pasta. Brush the egg wash around each mound of filling. Cover with the remaining 3 pasta sheets and use a fluted pasta wheel or knife to cut 2-inch (5-cm) squares around the mounds of filling. Seal the edges by pressing together by hand or with the tines of a fork. Arrange the ravioli on a platter and dust with flour on both sides so they do not stick. Refrigerate until ready to serve.

In a small, heavy skillet over medium-high heat, heat the canola oil and sauté the ginger strips until they start to brown. Using a slotted spoon, transfer the ginger to paper towels to drain.

In a medium sauté pan or skillet, melt the butter over medium heat. Add the tomatoes and stock or broth and cook for 5 minutes. Stir in the tarragon and salt and pepper to taste. Set aside and keep warm.

In a large pot of salted boiling water, cook the ravioli until al dente, 3 to 4 minutes; drain. Divide the ravioli among 6 plates. Spoon the tomato sauce over each portion. Top with ginger frizzles and serve immediately.

Makes 6 servings

■ Halibut with Broccoli ■
Filetti di Pesce con Broccoli

Bread crumbs seasoned with fresh herbs are one of Francesco Antonucci's favorite touches for dressing up a variety of dishes. This handsome dish, with broccoli adorning the fish in its browned crust, could be served with mashed potatoes.

1 cup (2 oz/60 g) small broccoli florets

¼ cup (½ oz/15 g) fresh bread crumbs (see Basics)

2 teaspoons minced fresh sage

8 tablespoons (4 fl oz/125 ml) extra-virgin olive oil

4 halibut fillets, about 1½ pounds (75 g) total

½ cup (4 fl oz/125 ml) fish stock (see Basics) or canned low-salt chicken broth

⅓ cup (3 fl oz/80 ml) fresh lemon juice

Salt and freshly ground pepper to taste

Steam the broccoli over rapidly simmering water in a covered steamer until just tender, about 5 minutes. Immerse in ice water to stop the cooking process; drain and set aside. In a small bowl, mix the bread crumbs with 1 teaspoon of the sage. Coat the halibut fillets with the crumbs.

In a large sauté pan or skillet over medium heat, heat 3 tablespoons of the olive oil and sauté the halibut for about 5 minutes on each side, or until browned on the outside and opaque throughout. Transfer to a serving dish and cover to keep warm.

Add the remaining 5 tablespoons olive oil, the stock or broth, and lemon juice to the skillet. Stir in the broccoli and remaining 1 teaspoon sage and cook to reheat the broccoli. Season with salt and pepper. Arrange a halibut steak on each of 4 warmed plates, spoon the broccoli and sauce around the fish, and serve immediately.

Makes 4 servings

■ Apple-Mascarpone Tart ■
Torta di Mele e Mascarpone

4 prunes

1 tablespoon Armagnac or brandy

Sweet Pastry Dough with Walnuts

1¾ cups (9 oz/280 g) all-purpose flour

¾ cup (3 oz/90 g) powdered sugar

¾ cup (3 oz/90 g) walnuts, toasted and ground (see Basics)

½ teaspoon salt

⅔ cup (5 oz/155 g) cold butter, cut into small cubes

1 egg, beaten

½ teaspoon vanilla extract

¼ cup (2 oz/60 g) butter

1 cinnamon stick

¼ cup (3 oz/90 g) maple syrup

4 Granny Smith or Golden Delicious apples, peeled, cored, and diced

½ teaspoon salt

Mascarpone-Sour Cream Mixture

¼ cup (2 oz/60 g) mascarpone at room temperature

¼ cup (2 oz/60 g) sour cream

¼ cup (2 oz/60 g) granulated sugar

3 eggs, beaten

Grated zest of ½ orange

In a small bowl, combine the prunes and hot water to cover. Soak for 5 minutes. Drain the prunes and chop coarsely. Transfer to a small bowl and add the Armagnac or brandy. Set aside for at least 4 hours.

To make the pastry dough: In a medium bowl, stir the flour, sugar, walnuts, and salt together until blended. Using a pastry cutter or 2 knives, cut in the butter to make pea-sized crumbs. Stir in the egg and vanilla and mix quickly until the dough just forms a ball. Flatten the dough into a disk, cover with plastic wrap, and refrigerate for at least 45 minutes. On a lightly floured work surface, roll the dough out until ⅛-inch thick and transfer to a 9-inch (23-cm) tart pan with a removable bottom. Roll the rolling pin over the top of the pan to trim the dough. Prick the bottom of the pastry with a fork and refrigerate for 30 minutes.

Preheat the oven to 375°F (190°C). Line the pastry with aluminum foil and fill with dried beans or pastry weights. Bake in the preheated oven for 20 minutes, or until lightly golden. Remove the beans or weights and foil.

In a large skillet, combine the butter, cinnamon stick, and maple syrup; stir over medium-low heat until the butter melts. Add the apples and cook, stirring occasionally, for 15 minutes, or until they are tender but still hold their shape. Stir in the salt. Set aside to cool.

In a medium bowl, combine the mascarpone, sour cream, sugar, eggs, and orange zest; stir until well mixed.

Preheat the oven to 425°F (220°C). Using a slotted spoon, transfer the apples to the tart shell and arrange them in an even layer. Sprinkle over the reserved prunes. Pour in the mascarpone mixture and bake in the lower third of the preheated oven for 15 minutes, or until puffed and golden. Serve warm or at room temperature.

Make 8 to 10 servings

CRISTOFORO MUNARI. Still Life with Fruit. Galleria Estense, Modena, Italy

SAN DOMENICO

New York, New York

Tony May opened San Domenico NY in 1988, and the restaurant still sets the standard for classic and contemporary Italian cuisine in the United States. As Chairman of Gruppo Ristoratori Italiani and a Board Member of DIRONA, May has been at the forefront of efforts in the United States and Italy to foster a more complete understanding of Italian food and wine. He also serves on the board of the Culinary Institute of America, where he was active in establishing the Caterina de' Medici restaurant and a course teaching authentic Italian cooking to American students. May travels frequently to Italy to gather new ideas for San Domenico's ambitious and constantly evolving menu.

Located across from Central Park and just a few blocks south of Lincoln Center, San Domenico is the perfect setting in which to enjoy a luxurious, slow meal. The dining room's sleek lines, terra-cotta colors, burnished woods, and marble floors exemplify classic Italian style and establish a light and relaxing environment. May and his daughter Marisa preside in the dining room, greeting guests and graciously stopping to chat at every table.

Executive chef Odette Fada, who has been in charge of the kitchen since 1996, developed her skills while working at a number of restaurants in Italy, including as chef de cuisine at Convivo Vissani in Rome. She introduced Los Angeles to her refined cooking style at the highly acclaimed Rex il Ristorante. Chef Fada is currently placing her own stamp on San Domenico's list of seasonal dishes and giving her customers the experience of impressive new tastes from her native Italy. Diners may order the chef's menu de gustazione or enjoy fixed-price lunch and dinner menus. The wine cellar at San Domenico houses a celebrated collection of wines from Italy, California, and the Pacific Norhwest.

MENU

Squab Salad
Insalata di Piccione

Risotto with Scampi
Risotto agli Scampi

Poached Sea Bass in Herbed Tomato Broth
Branzino all' Acqua Pazza

Chocolate Polenta Cakes
Polenta Nera

▪ Squab Salad ▪

Insalata di Piccione

An inspired mélange of flavors. If squab is unavailable, 3 Cornish hens or 6 quail may be substituted.

3 squabs, boned, legs separated from breasts

Salt and freshly ground pepper to taste

6 tablespoons (3 fl oz/80 ml) extra-virgin olive oil

2 tablespoons golden raisins

½ small butternut squash, peeled, seeded, and cut crosswise into thin slices

6 small handfuls mâche or mixed baby salad greens

1 tablespoon unsalted butter

Season the squab with salt and pepper. In a large sauté pan or skillet over medium heat, heat 2 tablespoons of the olive oil and sauté the squab, turning frequently, for 20 minutes, or until done. Test for doneness by inserting a sharp knife into the thigh. If the juices are pink, it needs to cook longer. If the juices run clear, it is done. Transfer the breasts to a cutting board and continue cooking the legs 2 or 3 minutes longer. Remove the legs.

In small bowl, combine the raisins with boiling water to cover; soak for 5 minutes, or until they are soft and plump; drain.

In a large pot of salted boiling water, cook the squash slices until easily pierced with a knife; drain.

In a medium bowl, combine the mâche or baby greens, salt, and remaining 4 tablespoons olive oil, and toss until well coated. Cut the squash slices in half and arrange them as fans on one side of each of 6 plates. On the other side of each plate, arrange a small mound of salad. Cut the breasts into thin slices. Arrange the slices of squab breast and the legs over the squash.

In a small sauté pan or skillet, melt the butter over medium heat and sauté the raisins for 2 minutes. Sprinkle the raisins over each plate, drizzle the butter over the squab, and serve.

Makes 6 servings

■ Risotto with Scampi ■
Risotto agli Scampi

Vialone Nano, Carnaroli, and Arborio rice are the best choices for risotto because of their ability to absorb liquid and cook to a creamy smoothness while still remaining firm to the bite. Scampi is not readily available in U.S. markets, so substitute large shrimp.

Shrimp Stock

24 large shrimp

3 tablespoons extra-virgin olive oil

⅓ cup (3 fl oz/80 ml) brandy

1 celery stalk, chopped

1 carrot, peeled and chopped

1 large onion, chopped

1 leek (white part only), chopped

4 Roma (plum) tomatoes, chopped

2 sprigs each fresh parsley, oregano, rosemary, and basil

4 garlic cloves, crushed

Pinch of red pepper flakes

4 black peppercorns

4 quarts (4 l) water

Salt and freshly ground pepper to taste

4 tablespoons (2 fl oz/60 ml) extra-virgin olive oil

2 shallots, minced

3 cups (21 oz/655 g) Vialone Nano, Carnaroli, or Aborio rice

½ cup (2 oz/60 g) freshly grated pecorino romano cheese

Chopped fresh flat-leaf parsley to taste

To make the shrimp stock: Shell and devein the shrimp and cut each into 5 or 6 pieces; reserve the heads and shells. In a large pot over medium heat, heat the olive oil and sauté the heads and shells until pink. Pour in the brandy. Using a long-handled match, ignite. When the flames have subsided, add the celery, carrot, onion, leek, tomatoes, herbs, garlic, pepper flakes, and peppercorns. Cook for 10 minutes, stirring constantly. Add the water, bring to a boil, reduce heat to low, and simmer for 2 hours. Remove from heat and let cool. Strain through a fine-meshed sieve, pushing the solids through with the back of a large spoon into a saucepan over medium-low heat. Season with salt and pepper. Return to the pot and bring to a low simmer.

In a large, heavy saucepan, heat 2 tablespoons of the olive oil and sauté the shallots until translucent, about 2 minutes. Add the rice and stir until well coated, about 2 minutes. Add ½ cup (4 fl oz/125 ml) of the shrimp stock and stir constantly until absorbed. Repeat the process until the rice is tender but firm, about 20 minutes. Stir in the shrimp, cheese, the remaining 2 tablespoons olive oil, and the parsley. Serve immediately in warmed pasta bowls.

Makes 6 servings

*Vialone Nano, Carnaroli, and Arborio rice are available at Italian markets and specialty foods stores.

■ Poached Sea Bass ■
in Herbed Tomato Broth

Branzino all'Acqua Pazza

This classic Neapolitan-style dish is called "Sea Bass in Crazy Water" in Italian. The name is derived from the "crazy" way the cooking water is transformed into a flavorful herbal tomato broth. At San Domenico, it is one of Luciano Pavarotti's favorite dishes.

Acqua Pazza Broth

2 tablespoons olive oil

½ small onion, chopped

2 garlic cloves, crushed

Pinch of red pepper flakes

1 fresh parsley sprig

½ bay leaf

Bones from 2 sea bass or striped bass (about 2 pounds each)

¼ cup dry white wine

6 Roma (plum) tomatoes, seeded and quartered

8 cups (64 fl oz/2 l) fish stock (see Basics)

2 slices firm-textured Italian or French bread, crusts trimmed

4 sea bass or striped bass fillets, halved

Salt and freshly ground pepper to taste

1 tablespoon extra-virgin olive oil, plus more for drizzling

2 garlic cloves, minced

2 tomatoes, peeled and diced (see Basics)

Pinch of red pepper flakes

2 zucchini, thinly sliced into small diamonds (1 inch/2.5 cm across)

Minced fresh flat-leaf parsley to taste

To make the acqua pazza broth: In a large pot over medium heat, heat the olive oil and sauté the onion until translucent, about 3 minutes. Add the garlic, pepper flakes, parsley, bay leaf, and fish bones. Pour in the white wine and stir to scrape up the browned bits on the bottom of the pan. Cook for about 5 minutes. Stir in the tomatoes and cook 5 minutes longer. Pour in the fish stock and bring to a boil. Reduce heat to low and simmer for 20 minutes. Strain the broth through a fine-meshed sieve. Reserve 2½ cups of the broth; freeze the rest.

Preheat the oven to 450°F (230°C). Cut each slice of bread into two 2-inch (5-cm) triangles, place on a baking sheet, and toast in the preheated oven for 8 minutes, or until golden brown; set aside.

Increase the oven temperature to 500°F (260°C). Season the fish fillets with salt and pepper. In an large ovenproof sauté pan or skillet over high heat, heat the olive oil and sauté the garlic for 2 minutes. Add the tomatoes and pepper flakes and cook for 5 minutes. Pour in the reserved 2½ cups (20 fl oz/625 ml) acqua pazza broth and bring to a boil. Add the zucchini and cook for 2 minutes, or until crisp-tender. Add the fish pieces and bake in the preheated oven for 3 minutes, or until opaque throughout. Using a slotted spoon, transfer the fish to a platter and cover to keep warm. Stir the parsley into the aqua pazza broth and drizzle with extra-virgin olive oil.

To serve: Place 2 fish pieces in each of 4 warmed shallow soup bowls, one on top of the other. Cover with vegetables and ladle in about ½ cup (4 fl oz/125 ml) of the aqua pazza broth. Top each serving with a crouton and serve immediately.

Makes 4 servings

■ Chocolate Polenta Cakes ■
Polenta Nera

These fabulous light cakes of chocolate, polenta, and hazelnuts are San Domenico's signature dessert. At the restaurant, each is served on a pool of white chocolate sauce.

8 ounces (125 g) bittersweet chocolate, chopped

2 tablespoons hazelnut paste*

4 tablespoons (2 oz/60 g) butter

¼ cup (1½ oz/45 g) polenta

½ cup (4 fl oz/125 ml) milk

3 egg yolks

1 teaspoon vanilla extract

4 egg whites

¼ cup sugar

Preheat the oven to 375°F (190°C). Butter six 3-inch (7.5-cm) ramekins and sprinkle with sugar; knock out the excess sugar. Melt the chocolate in a double boiler over barely simmering water. Stir in the hazelnut paste and set aside.

In a small saucepan, melt the butter over medium heat and gradually stir in the polenta; cook for 2 minutes, stirring constantly. Stir in the milk, reduce heat to low, and simmer, stirring frequently, for 30 minutes. Stir the chocolate mixture into the polenta. Beat in the egg yolks, one at a time, and stir in the vanilla. Transfer the mixture to a large bowl.

In a large bowl, beat the egg whites until foamy. Gradually beat in the sugar until stiff, glossy peaks form. Fold the whites into the polenta mixture. Spoon the batter into the prepared ramekins, filling them three-fourths full. Place the ramekins in a baking dish and add warm water to come halfway up the sides of the ramekins. Bake in the preheated oven for 20 minutes, or until a knife inserted in the center of a cake comes out clean. Serve warm.

Makes 6 servings

*Hazelnut paste is available at specialty foods stores, including Buon Italia in Manhattan; phone (212) 633-9090, fax (212) 633-9717.

GIOVANNA GARZONI. A Dish with Cherries and Carnations. Galleria Palatina,
Palazzo Pitti,Florence, Italy

IL SOLE DI RANCO

Ranco, Italy

An enchanting road in Lombardy runs past picturesque harbors, half-hidden villas, and luxuriant gardens along the shores of magnificent Lake Maggiore to the peaceful fishing village of Ranco. Here, five generations of the Brovelli family have transformed a small inn opened in 1872 into a restaurant acclaimed around the world. Il Sole di Ranco is a member of the prestigious Relais & Chateaux association.

Carlo Brovelli, Carluccio to his friends, is the master chef who has transformed Il Sole's kitchen. During a lifetime of sustained enthusiasm, dedication, and unstinting work, Brovelli has overcome countless difficulties to win international acclaim. Having cooked in Switzerland, France, and Germany, he has brought that experience, along with his own desire for excellence and artistic innovation, to the traditional cooking methods of Lombardy. The Brovellis' eldest son, Davide, works alongside his father in the kitchen, sharing his passion for quality and innovation. Davide Brovelli studied in France with Roger Vergé and worked in Los Angeles at Piero Selvaggio's Valentino and Primi restaurants. At Il Sole di Ranco, diners experience extraordinary home cooking by a family for its guests.

Carlo Brovelli has revived some of the lesser-known specialties of his native region, and many of his artistically presented dishes feature fish from Lake Maggiore, game birds such as wild duck and squab, and locally grown herbs. Each day Brovelli rolls out fabulous fresh pasta, including sheets striped green, red, and black with spinach purée, tomato purée, and black squid ink. Itala Brovelli, Carlo's wife, is the restaurant's expert sommelier. She presides in the art-filled dining room, graciously stopping to chat at every table. During summer months, dinners are enjoyed outside under a magnificent pergola overlooking the garden and the lake. Service is professional, friendly, and multilingual. The wine cellar contains Itala Brovelli's extensive selection of fine Italian, French, and California wines.

Adjoining the restaurant are fifteen comfortable suites with romantic views across the sailboat-dotted lake to the majestic snowcapped mountain peaks of the Alps. In the breakfast room or under the pergola, guests enjoy breakfasts that include a choice of yogurts, warm cakes, pastries, cooked fruits, homemade jams and marmalades, teas, coffee, and chocolate. Boat rides can be arranged, as well as visits to villas with Italian and English gardens and tours of nearby fortresses, towers, and castles. Chef Carlo Brovelli created the following recipes and presented them to Menus and Music.

Then the pernicious charm of Italy worked on her, and instead of acquiring information, she began to be happy.

—E. M. Forster, A Room With a View

MENU

Trout and Perch Carpaccio
Carpaccio di Trota e Persico

Lasagna with Sea Bass and Basil Butter
La Lasagna del "Sole" con Branzino e Burro al Basilico

Roasted Sturgeon with Herbs
Storione alle Erbe Arrosto

Caramelized Squab with Honey
Piccione Caramellato al Miele

Sicilian-Style Cassata with Raspberry Sauce
Cassata alla Siciliana con Salsa al Lampone

■ Trout and Perch Carpaccio ■
Carpaccio di Trota e Persico

Paper-thin pinwheel slices of pink and white fish fillets are dressed with pepper oil for a pretty, delicate-flavored first course. Choose fillets of about the same size and the freshest fish possible, since it will be served raw. Drink a Pinot Grigio or a sparkling Franciacorta Brut.

1 red trout fillet, skinless

2 large perch or sole fillets

Salt and freshly ground pepper to taste

Pepper Oil

½ cup (4 fl oz/125 ml) extra-virgin olive oil

½ tablespoon pink peppercorns

Pinch of salt

4 small handfuls mixed salad greens, lightly dressed with vinaigrette (see Basics)

1 tablespoon caviar (optional)

Sprinkle the fish fillets with salt and pepper. On a plate, lay out one of the perch or sole fillets, top it with the trout fillet and then the remaining perch or sole fillet. Working from one long side, gently roll the fillets. Using kitchen string, tie the roll tightly. Cover and refrigerate overnight.

In a blender or food processor, combine the olive oil, peppercorns, and salt; process until smooth.

Using a very sharp large knife, slice the chilled fish roll into paper-thin slices. On each of 4 plates, arrange the pinwheel slices in the shape of a flower to cover each plate. Arrange a small mound of salad in the center and drizzle the fish with the pepper oil. Sprinkle with caviar, if you wish, and serve immediately.

Makes 4 servings

■ Lasagna with Sea Bass ■ and Basil Butter

La Lasagna del "Sole" con Branzino e Burro al Basilico

At Il Sole di Ranco, chef Carlo Brovelli uses spinach, tomato, and squid ink to create a spectacular green, red, and black striped pasta for this dish. In this recipe, sheets plain egg pasta, cut into squares, cover steamed sea bass or shrimp dressed with a flavorful basil butter.

Pasta

3¼ cups (16 oz/500 g) all-purpose flour

2 eggs

6 egg yolks

Pinch of salt

2 tablespoons extra-virgin olive oil

Basil Butter

2 cups (16 fl oz/500 ml) water

1 small bunch fresh basil, stemmed

1 tablespoon beef broth (see Basics), canned low-salt beef broth, or water

7 tablespoons (3½ oz/105 g) butter at room temperature

4 sea bass fillets, halved, or 12 large shimp, shelled and deveined

Salt and freshly ground pepper to taste

To make the pasta: Pour the flour into a mound on a work surface and make a well in the center. Add the eggs, egg yolks, salt, and olive oil to the well. Using a fork, beat the eggs, yolks, salt, and olive oil just until blended. Begin mixing the flour into the egg mixture, drawing the flour from the inside wall of the well until a dough is formed. Alternatively, combine the ingredients in a food processor and process just until a ball is formed. On a floured work surface, knead the dough until smooth and elastic, about 8 minutes. Divide the pasta into 4 equal parts, cover with plastic wrap, and set aside for 30 minutes.

Set the rollers of a pasta machine at the highest number. (The rollers will be wide apart.) Flatten one piece of dough into a rough rectangle. Feed the pasta through the rollers. Fold the rectangle in half and feed through the rollers 8 or 9 more times, folding the dough in half each time and dusting it with flour if necessary to prevent sticking. Turn the dial down one notch and feed the dough through the rollers without folding. Continue to feed the dough through the rollers without folding, turning the dial one notch lower each time until the lowest or second-lowest notch is reached. The dough will be a smooth long sheet, 4 to 5 inches (10 to 13 cm) wide and about 1/16 inch (2 mm) thick. Cut the lasagna into eight 4½-inch (11.5-cm) squares.

In a large pot of boiling salted water, drop in the lasagna squares one by one. Cook for about 3 minutes, or the water returns to a boil and the pasta floats to the top. Using a large slotted spoon in one hand and a fork in the other, lift out the lasagna squares and drain. Rinse in cold water and spread out on clean towels. Do not stack the pieces because they may stick together.

To make the butter: In a small saucepan, combine the water, 5 of the basil leaves, and the broth or water. Bring to a boil and cook until the liquid is reduced to 1 cup. Remove the basil leaves. In a food processor, purée the remaining basil. Add the basil purée to the liquid. Whisk in the butter until blended. Set aside and keep warm.

Steam the sea bass or shrimp over simmering water in a covered steamer for about 5 minutes, or until the fish is opaque throughout or the shrimp is evenly pink. Place a square of lasagna in the center of each of 4 warmed plates. Top with a piece of sea bass or 3 shrimp, season with salt and pepper, and drizzle the basil butter over. Cover with a second lasagna square, slightly offset. Drizzle over a little basil butter and serve immediately.

Makes 4 servings

▪ Roasted Sturgeon with Herbs ▪

Storione alle Erbe Arrosto

Since the sixth century, cooks in Lombardy have been using earthenware roasters to cook flavorful poultry and fish dishes. Here, sturgeon is roasted to perfection in earthenware or a casserole with a tight-fitting lid and flavored with herbs and green hay or hazelnuts. This dish was prepared by Il Sole di Ranco at the Metropolitan Opera House in New York for Tutta Italia, a charity benefit organized by City Meals on Wheels.

1 cup (8 fl oz/250 ml) extra-virgin olive oil

Juice of 1 lemon

1 fresh fennel sprig

5 fresh lemon verbena leaves

1 fresh marjoram sprig

1 fresh thyme sprig

1 fresh oregano sprig

4 sturgeon fillets, cut into 16 large bite-sized pieces

Salt and freshly ground pepper to taste

2 large handfuls green hay, or 2 cups (8 oz/250 g) hazelnuts, toasted and skinned (see Basics)

Garnish

2 bunches dandelion leaves or arugula, stemmed

4 handfuls mixed salad greens

6 tablespoons (3 fl oz/80 ml) vinaigrette (see Basics)

2 tomatoes, peeled, seeded, and diced (see Basics)

2 tablespoons small capers

8 fresh basil leaves

In a large, shallow bowl, whisk the olive oil and lemon juice together. Stir in the fennel, lemon verbena, marjoram, thyme, and oregano. Add the fish pieces, salt, and pepper. Set aside to marinate for about 40 minutes.

Preheat the oven to 350°F (180°C). Arrange half of the hay or hazelnuts in the bottom of an earthenware roaster (follow the manufacturer's instructions) or a casserole with a tight-fitting lid; sprinkle the hay, if using, with a little water. Drain the fish pieces and arrange them over the hay or hazelnuts. Cover with the remaining hay or hazelnuts; again sprinkle the hay, if using, with water. Cover the casserole or roaster tightly and bake in the preheated oven for 25 minutes. Remove from the oven and set aside to cool for 15 minutes.

In a medium bowl, toss the dandelion or arugula and salad greens with the vinaigrette. Arrange a nest of salad on each of 4 plates. Place 4 sturgeon pieces on top of each salad and sprinkle with the tomatoes, capers, and basil. Serve immediately.

Makes 4 servings

■ Caramelized Squab with Honey ■

Piccione Caramellato al Miele

Four Cornish hens or 8 quail may be substituted for the squab. Use Italian acacia honey (see Resources) or another flavorful honey for this dish.

4 meaty squab, halved

2 garlic cloves, halved

4 tablespoons (2 fl oz/60 ml) extra-virgin olive oil

¼ cup (3 oz/90 g) honey, warmed

1 teaspoon minced fresh thyme

½ teaspoon ground cloves

Salt and freshly ground pepper to taste

4 tablespoons (2 oz/60 g) butter

1 cup (8 fl oz/250 ml) aged balsamic vinegar

1½ cups (6 oz/185 g) cherries, stems cut ½ inch (12 mm) from the fruit, or green seedless grapes

½ white cabbage, cored and shredded

Rub the squab with the cut garlic, then with 2 tablespoons of the olive oil. Coat with the honey. Sprinkle with the thyme, cloves, salt, and pepper. Pierce the meat with a fork all over to help all the flavors penetrate into the meat. Set aside for about 30 minutes to marinate.

In a small saucepan, bring the balsamic vinegar to a boil, add the cherries or grapes, and immediately remove from heat. Cover and let the fruit macerate for at least 1 hour.

In 2 large sauté pans or skillets, melt the butter over low heat and sauté the squab, turning frequently, for about 1 hour, or until well browned on all sides on the outside and rare on the inside. Test for doneness by inserting a sharp knife into the thigh. If the juices run pink, it needs to cook longer. If the juices run clear, it is done. Cover and set aside.

Return the saucepan with the fruit to medium heat until the cherries or grapes are just heated through.

Toss the cabbage with the remaining 2 tablespoons olive oil. Add salt and pepper to taste and toss again. Place the squab and a mound of cabbage salad on each of 4 plates. Serve the warm cherries or grapes alongside.

Makes 4 servings

■ Sicilian-Style Cassata ■ with Raspberry Sauce

Cassata alla Siciliana con Salsa al Lampone

Il Sole di Ranco's version of cassata, the traditional Sicilian dessert of sponge cake, ice cream, and candied fruit, is served in individual molds. The dessert may also be made in one large mold.

Vanilla Gelato

6 egg yolks

¾ cup (6 oz/185 g) sugar

2 tablespoons water

2 cups (16 fl oz/500 ml) milk

1 vanilla bean, split lengthwise, or 1 teaspoon vanilla extract

Grated zest of 1 lemon

2 egg whites

5 tablespoons (3 oz/90 g) sugar

¼ cup (2 fl oz/60 ml) heavy (whipping) cream

¼ cup (1½ oz/45 g) finely diced candied fruit, macerated in rum

½ sponge cake, sliced into ½-inch-wide strips (see Basics)

Raspberrry Sauce

2 cups (8 oz/250 g) fresh raspberries, or 10 ounces (315 g) thawed frozen unsweetened raspberries

Powdered sugar to taste

To make the gelato: In a medium bowl, whisk the egg yolks and sugar together until foamy; set aside.

In a medium saucepan, bring the milk, vanilla bean, if using, and lemon zest just to a boil; remove from heat, cover, and set aside for 15 minutes. Whisk the egg mixture into the milk mixture. Return to very low heat and whisk constantly until thick enough to coat a spoon, about 10 minutes; do not boil. Remove from heat and stir in the vanilla extract, if using; remove the vanilla bean, if using. Transfer to a bowl, and let cool. Cover and refrigerate until chilled, about 2 hours. Freeze in an ice cream maker according to the manufacturer's instructions.

In a large bowl, beat the egg whites until soft peaks form. In a small, heavy saucepan, combine the sugar and water without stirring and cook over medium heat until the sugar dissolves, about 4 minutes. Increase heat to medium-high and cook until a candy thermometer registers 234°F (117°C) degrees, the soft-ball stage.

Gradually beat the sugar syrup in a thin steady stream into the egg whites (without pouring the syrup over the beaters or the sides of the bowl) until the mixture is glossy, doubled in volume, and cooled to room temperature, 4 to 5 minutes.

In a deep bowl, beat the cream until stiff peaks form. Using a rubber spatula, fold in the egg white mixture, candied fruit, and ice cream.

Line four 3-inch-diameter (7.5-cm) molds or ramekins with sponge cake strips and fill with the cream mixture. Cover the molds with plastic wrap and freeze for 3 or 4 hours before unmolding.

In a blender or food processor, combine the raspberries and powdered sugar and process until puréed.

To serve, spoon a pool of raspberry sauce onto each of 4 dessert plates. Invert a cassata mold on top of each pool of sauce and serve immediately.

Makes 4 servings

SOTTO SOTTO

Atlanta, Georgia

Chef Riccardo Ullio established Sotto Sotto (which means "hush, hush" in Italian) in 1999, and it has been a challenge to get a table at his lively restauarant ever since. A native of Milan, the gifted young chef captures the essential tastes of his home country with fresh, direct cooking in a trim, contemporary setting.

At Sotto Sotto, you can start your meal with a tasting of estate-bottled olive oils from Italy's premier producing regions. Ullio's selection of silky, hand-rolled pastas include Tortelli di Michelangelo, "a faithful reproduction of the artist's favorite ravioli recipe" culled from a Michelangelo journal. Other highlights include shellfish risotto made with Carnaroli rice and wood-oven roasted whole fish or chicken.

Sotto Sotto's large storefront windows reveal chefs in white engaged in all the bustling activites that occur in a busy restaurant kitchen, as well as the restaurant's glowing wood-burning oven and sheets of fresh pasta stretched over a long wooden table. The understated open space of the sixty-eight-seat dining room makes it a perfect backdrop for the drama that unfolds here six nights a week, and the contemporary-design chairs, blue-bottomed glasses, and heavy white porcelain plates all come from Italy. Chef Riccardo Ullio presented Menus and Music with the following menu and recipes.

MENU

Neapolitan-Style Mussels

Impepata di Cozze

Celery and Black Truffle Salad

Insalata di Sedano e Tartufi

Spaghetti with Cheese and Pepper

Spaghetti Cacio e Pepe

Cooked Cream with Balsamic Vinegar

Panna Cotta all'Aceto Balsamico

■ Neapolitan-Style Mussels ■

Impepata di Cozze

This is Sotto Sotto's version of a traditional Neapolitan dish.

¼ cup (4 fl oz/125 ml) extra-virgin olive oil

8 garlic cloves, thinly sliced

4 pounds (2 kg) mussels, scrubbed and debearded

Freshly cracked pepper to taste

Pinch of salt

Juice of 2 lemons

¼ cup (⅓ oz/10 g) chopped fresh flat-leaf parsley

In a large skillet over high heat, combine the olive oil, garlic, and mussels and cook for 1 minute. Sprinkle generously with pepper and add the salt. Cover with a tightly fitting lid and cook until the mussels open, about 5 minutes. Discard any mussels that do not open.

Divide the mussels among 4 warmed shallow bowls. Squeeze the juice of half a lemon over each serving and sprinkle with parsley. Serve immediately.

Makes 4 servings

▪ Celery and Black Truffle Salad ▪

Insalata di Sedano e Tartufi

A dish that highlights the flavors of Umbria, where it would be made with celery from Trevi and black truffles from Spoleto.

Pinch of salt

2 tablespoons fresh lemon juice

½ cup (4 oz/120 ml) extra-virgin olive oil

Freshly cracked pepper to taste

2 golf ball-sized black truffles, shaved to about ¹⁄₁₆ inch (2 mm) thick

½ celery stalk, cut into ⅛-inch-thick (3-mm) diagonal slices

¼ cup (⅓ oz/10 g) coarsely shaved Parmesan cheese

In a medium bowl, whisk the salt and lemon juice together until the salt dissolves. Whisk in the olive oil and pepper. Add the truffles and celery. Toss very gently so as not to damage the truffles. Divide the salad among 4 plates and place a few Parmesan shavings on each serving.

Makes 4 servings

■ Spaghetti with Cheese and Pepper ■
Spaghetti Cacio e Pepe

2 tablespoons extra-virgin olive oil

8 ounces (250 g) pancetta or rindless bacon, cut into ½-inch (12-mm) dice

8 ounces (250 g) spaghetti

Salt and cracked black pepper to taste

2 cups (8 oz/250 g) freshly grated pecorino romano cheese

In a large sauté pan or skillet over low heat, heat the olive oil and sauté the pancetta or bacon until the fat is rendered. Increase heat to medium and cook until the pancetta or bacon browns. Pour off all but 1 tablespoon of the fat.

In a large pot of salted boiling water, cook the spaghetti until al dente, about 9 minutes. Drain, reserving ½ cup (4 fl oz/250 ml) of the pasta water.

Add the reserved pasta water to the pan with the pancetta or bacon and stir. Add the spaghetti and toss.

Divide the spaghetti among 4 warmed shallow bowls. Add the salt and sprinkle generously with the cracked pepper. Sprinkle with the cheese. Serve immediately.

Makes 4 servings

■ Cooked Cream with Balsamic Vinegar ■
Panna Cotta all'Aceto Balsamico

At Sotto Sotto, this silky, eggless custard is served with caramel sauce or balsamico extravecchio, vinegar that has been aged more than thirty years. Just a drizzle changes panna cotta into something sublime. This is a perfect dessert for dinner parties, as it can be made a day or two in advance.

2 envelopes plain gelatin

½ cup (4 fl oz/125 ml) cold water

4 cups (32 fl oz/1 l) heavy (whipping) cream

⅞ cup (7 oz/220 g) sugar

¼ cup (2 fl oz/60 ml) white rum

¼ teaspoon grated lemon zest

½ vanilla bean, split lengthwise, or 1 teaspoon vanilla extract

8 coffee beans

2 teaspoons Aceto Balsamico Tradizionale di Modena*
  for drizzling

Sprinkle the gelatin over the water and let soak for 3 minutes. Meanwhile, in a large saucepan, combine the cream, sugar, rum, lemon zest, vanilla bean (if using), and coffee beans. Heat over medium heat to almost boiling. Remove from heat and strain through a fine-meshed sieve into a medium bowl. Stir in the gelatin mixture and the vanilla extract, if using. Pour the cream mixture into eight ½-cup (4-fl oz/250-ml) molds or ramekins. Refrigerate for at least 3 hours before serving.

To serve, fill a medium skillet with 1 inch (2.5 cm) of water and bring to a simmer. Use a knife to loosen the sides of the molds or ramekins. Place each in the simmering water for 1 or 2 seconds, then invert on a plate to unmold. Drizzle each panna cotta with ¼ teaspoon balsamic vinegar.

Makes 8 servings

*Aceto Balsamico Tradizionale di Modena is a highly prized and highly concentrated sweet, dark vinegar, really a condiment, which is aged at least twelve years in wooden casks. Its production is regulated by a producer's consortium. Extravecchio balsamic is aged thirty years or more. Aceto Balsamico di Modena is the legal designation of the better imitations.

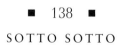

SOTTO SOTTO

CARAVAGGIO. Fruit Basket. Pinacoteca Ambrosiana, Milan, Italy

Greens and fruit the color of the loveliest
time of year. Some baskets which display
the pulps, sweet, fresh, and raw, tempting to desire.

Erbe, frutta colori della bella
stagione. Poche ceste ove alla sete
si rivelano dolci polpe crude.

—Umberto Saba, from "Fruits and Vegetables"

SPIAGGIA

Chicago, Illinois

Considered a culinary treasure not just in the Chicago area, but throughout the United States, Spiaggia features the extraordinary cooking of executive chef and managing partner Paul Bartolotta. His vibrant seasonal menus celebrate unusually fine ingredients, complex flavors, and the elegant simplicity of nothing-to-hide presentation. A recipient of a James Beard Award, Bartolotta was awarded the Insegna del Ristorante Italiano del Mondo in 1997 by the president of Italy for his achievement in the culinary arts and for being a goodwill ambassador for all things Italian.

The name Spiaggia, which means "beach" in Italian, was inspired by the restaurant's spectacular view of Lake Michigan. Floor-to-ceiling windows and the careful arrangement of tables result in a splendid environment in which to enjoy a luxurious, relaxed meal. Every detail of the restaurant has been thoughtfully orchestrated and chosen to add to a memorable dining experience. Chef Bartolotta, who has been in charge of the kitchen since 1991, developed his skills and creativity during a seven-year education in Italy, where he dined at almost every important Italian restaurant and learned the subtleties of *alta cucina* while working at the acclaimed San Domenico restaurant near Bologna. Bartolotta returned to the United States to work with Tony May at Palio under chef Andrea Hellrigl and was chef at New York's San Domenico from 1988 to 1991. Chef Paul Bartolotta created the following menu and recipes and presented them to Menus and Music.

MENU

■■■■■■■■■■

Sea Scallops with Belgian Endive

Cappesante Dorate con Endivia Belga

Tuscan Mussel Soup with White Beans

Guazzetto di Cozze e Cannellini

Goat's Milk Robiola Cappellacci
in a Creamy Tomato and Basil Sauce with Speck

Cappellacci di Robiola con Speck

Lamb Chops
with Balsamic Vinegar Glaze

Agnello all'Aceto Balsamico

Warm Fruit Soup Scented with Mint

Macedonia di Frutta Calda con Gelato alla Menta

■ Sea Scallops with Belgian Endive ■

Cappesante Dorate con Endivia Belga

This pretty star-shaped salad makes an impressive yet quickly prepared first course.

½ cup (4 fl oz/250 ml) plus 2 tablespoons extra-virgin olive oil

Juice of 2 lemons

Salt and freshly ground pepper to taste

20 endive leaves

20 sea scallops

2 tablespoons chopped fresh chives

2 tablespoons finely diced tomatoes

In a small bowl, whisk the ½ cup (4 fl oz/250 ml) olive oil, lemon juice, salt, and pepper together until emulsified; set aside.

In a large sauté pan or skillet over medium heat, heat 1 tablespoon of the remaining olive oil and sauté the endive leaves until golden, about 3 minutes. Arrange 5 endive leaves in a star pattern on each of 4 plates, leaving room in the center for 4 scallops.

Clean the pan with a paper towel and return it to medium-high heat. Season the scallops with salt and pepper to taste. Add the remaining 1 tablespoon olive oil and sauté the scallops until golden brown, about 2 minutes on each side. Arrange 4 scallops in the center of each endive star and place 1 scallop on top.

Spoon about 1½ tablespoons vinaigrette over the scallops on each plate and drizzle the vinaigrette over the endive leaves. Sprinkle the entire plate with chives and diced tomatoes.

Makes 4 servings

Tuscan Mussel Soup with White Beans

Guazzetto di Cozze e Cannellini

Four 1-inch (2.5-cm) cubes firm-textured Italian or French bread

1 garlic clove, halved

Extra-virgin olive oil for drizzling, plus 4 teaspoons

Salt to taste

2 teaspoons butter

2 teaspoons minced garlic

2 bay leaves

48 mussels, scrubbed and debearded

1½ cups (12 fl oz/375 ml) dry white wine

Pinch of red pepper flakes

½ cup (4 oz/125 ml) bean broth or chicken broth (see Basics) or
   canned low-salt chicken broth

½ cup (3½ oz/105 g) cooked cannellini beans

4 tomatoes, peeled, seeded, and diced (see Basics)

4 teaspoons minced fresh flat-leaf parsley

Freshly ground white pepper to taste

Preheat the oven to 450°F (230°C). Put the bread cubes on a baking sheet and toast in the preheated oven for 8 minutes, or until golden. Rub the croutons with the garlic clove, drizzle with olive oil, and sprinkle with salt.

In a large saucepan, melt the butter with the 4 teaspoons olive oil over medium heat and sauté the garlic and bay leaves for 2 minutes; do not let the garlic brown. Add the mussels, white wine, and pepper flakes; cover and bring to a boil. Cook until the mussels open, about 5 minutes. Discard any mussels that do not open.

Using a slotted spoon, transfer the mussels to a plate and remove the mussels from the shells. Add the bean broth or chicken broth to the mussel broth and bring to a boil. Add the beans, tomatoes, parsley, pepper, and salt to taste. Add the mussels and cook for 1 or 2 minutes just to heat through. Place a bread crouton in the bottom of each of 4 shallow soup bowls, ladle in the soup, and serve hot.

Makes 4 servings

■ Goat's Milk Robiola Cappellacci ■ in a Creamy Tomato and Basil Sauce with Speck

Cappellacci di Robiola con Speck

Literally "shabby old hats," cappellacci are stuffed pasta triangles formed into ring shapes that resemble pointed hats. Fill with robiola, a mild, creamy Italian cheese with a fresh, refined taste, or a fresh goat cheese.

Pasta Dough

3¼ cups (1 pound/500 g) unbleached all-purpose flour

5 eggs

Pinch of salt

1 tablespoon water

Filling

12 ounces (375 g) goat's milk robiola or fresh white goat cheese at
  room temperature

Salt and freshly ground white pepper to taste

Sauce

4 tablespoons (2 oz/60 g) butter

20 fresh basil leaves, plus 4 fresh basil sprigs for garnish

2 tomatoes, peeled, seeded, and diced (see Basics)

1 cup (8 fl oz/250 ml) heavy (whipping) cream

32 thin strips speck* or bacon, chopped

¼ cup (1 oz/30 g) freshly grated Parmesan cheese

Salt to taste

To make the dough: Heap the flour into a mound on a flat work surface and make a well in the center. Break the eggs into it and add the salt and water. Using a fork, beat the eggs, salt, and water just to blend. Begin mixing the flour into the egg mixture, drawing the flour from the inside wall of the well until a dough is formed. Alternatively, add the flour, eggs, salt, and water to the bowl of a food processor and process just until a ball forms.

On a lightly floured work surface, knead the dough until smooth and elastic, about 8 minutes. Divide the dough in half, cover with plastic wrap, and let rest for at least 30 minutes before rolling out.

To make the filling: In a medium bowl, cream the robiola or goat cheese with the salt and pepper.

Set the rollers of a pasta machine at the highest number. Flatten one piece of the dough into a rough rectangle. Feed the rectangle through the rollers. Fold in half and feed through the rollers 8 or 9 more times, folding the dough in half each time and dusting with flour if necessary to prevent sticking. Turn the dial down one notch and feed the dough through the rollers without folding. Continue to feed the dough through the rollers without folding, turning the dial one notch lower each time until the second-lowest notch is reached. The dough will be a smooth long sheet, 4 to 5 inches (10 to 13 cm) wide.

Cut the pasta into 1½-inch (4-cm) squares. Put about ¼ teaspoon filling in the center of each square. Fold the square in half diagonally to form an offset triangle. The upper edges should not quite meet the lower; they should stop about ⅛ inch (3 mm) short. Press down firmly to seal the sides. Hold the triangle between your thumb and index finger, with the tip of the triangle pointing upward. Wrap the base around the index finger until the two ends meet; press the two ends firmly together. Repeat with the rest of the pasta and filling.

To make the sauce: In a medium sauté pan or skillet over medium heat, melt the butter with the 20 basil leaves. When the leaves are wilted, add the tomatoes and cook for about 3 minutes. Stir in the cream, speck or bacon, Parmesan, and salt.

In a large pot of boiling salted water, add the cappellacci and boil for 5 minutes, or until the water returns to a boil and the cappellacci float to the top. Gently drain and toss with the sauce in the pan until evenly coated. Divide the cappellacci among 4 shallow soup bowls. Garnish each plate with a fresh basil sprig and serve.

Makes 4 servings

*Speck is a fatty ham that is smoked with herbs and spices, then air-dried. It comes from the Tyrol near the Swiss border and once part of Bavaria, which explains its German-sounding name. Speck is available at Italian foods stores and specialty foods markets.

■ Lamb Chops ■
with Balsamic Vinegar Glaze
Agnello all'Aceto Balsamico

Lamb chops covered with a richly flavored mahogany glaze.

Potato-Cauliflower Purée

8 ounces (250 g) Yukon Gold potatoes

½ head cauliflower, cored and cut into small florets

½ cup (4 fl oz/125 ml) extra-virgin olive oil

Salt and freshly ground pepper to taste

12 loin lamb chops, trimmed of fat

Salt and freshly ground pepper to taste

½ cup (4 fl oz/125 ml) plus 1 tablespoon extra-virgin olive oil

3 tablespoons unsalted butter

2 garlic cloves, sliced

2 fresh rosemary sprigs, plus 4 fresh rosemary sprigs for garnish

¼ cup (2 fl oz/60 ml) red wine vinegar

½ cup (4 fl oz/125 ml) balsamic vinegar

2 tablespoons tomato paste

¼ cup (2 oz/60 g) crushed tomatoes

½ cup (4 fl oz/125 ml) chicken broth (see Basics) or canned
  low-salt chicken broth

To make the potato-cauliflower purée: Cook the potatoes in a large saucepan of salted boiling water for 20 to 30 minutes, or until tender when pierced with a fork. Peel and coarsely chop. Return to the saucepan and keep warm. Meanwhile, cook the cauliflower in salted boiling water for 10 minutes, or until tender; drain. Add the cauliflower, olive oil, salt, and pepper to the potatoes. Using a wooden spoon, mash the potatoes and cauliflower to make a chunky purée; set aside and keep warm. Season the lamb chops with salt and pepper. In a large sauté pan or skillet over high heat, coat the pan with olive oil and quickly brown the chops for 1 or 2 minutes on each side, working in batches as necessary; they will still be very rare in the center. Transfer the chops to a plate and set aside. Discard all the cooked oil.

Reduce heat to medium and add the 1 tablespoon olive oil and 1 tablespoon of the butter. Sauté the garlic and 2 rosemary sprigs for 2 minutes, or until the garlic is golden. Stir in the red wine vinegar, balsamic vinegar, tomato paste, and crushed tomatoes. Add the lamb chops and cook until they are medium rare, about 5 minutes. Transfer the chops to a plate and loosely cover with aluminum foil.

Raise heat to high, add the chicken broth, and cook to reduce the liquid by half. Strain through a fine-meshed sieve and return to high heat. Swirl in the remaining 2 tablespoons butter. Season with salt and freshly ground pepper to taste.

Arrange 3 lamb chops and a scoop of potato-cauliflower purée on each of 4 plates. Cover the chops with glaze, garnish with a rosemary sprig, and serve immediately.

Makes 4 servings

■ Warm Fruit Soup Scented with Mint ■

Macedonia di Frutta Calda con Gelato alla Menta

Berry Sauce

⅓ cup (1½ oz/45 g) fresh blueberries

⅓ cup (1½ oz/45 g) fresh blackberries

⅓ cup (1½ oz/45 g) fresh raspberries

⅓ cup (1½ oz/45 g) hulled fresh strawberries

½ cup (4 fl oz/125 ml) water

¼ cup (2 oz/60 g) sugar

2 tablespoons butter

¼ cup (2 oz/60 g) sugar, plus more if needed

16 fresh mint leaves, stacked and cut into fine strips

Juice of 1 lemon, plus more if needed

¾ cup (3 oz/90 g) fresh blueberries

¾ cup (3 oz/90 g) fresh blackberries

¾ cup (3 oz/90 g) fresh strawberries

¾ cup (3 oz/90 g) fresh raspberries

Vanilla or mint ice cream for serving

4 fresh mint sprigs for garnish

To make the berry sauce: In a blender or food processor, combine all the ingredients and process until smooth; set aside.

In a saucepan over medium heat, melt the butter and stir in the ¼ cup (2 oz/60 g) sugar and the mint. Add the berry sauce, lemon juice, and all the berries except the raspberries. Heat until almost boiling, then stir in the raspberries. Taste and, if necessary, add sugar and lemon juice to taste. Ladle the warm fruit soup into 4 serving bowls. Place 1 scoop of ice cream on top of each serving, garnish with a mint sprig, and serve immediately.

Makes 4 servings

IL TERRAZZO CARMINE

Seattle, Washington

Born in Naples, Carmine Esmeraldo is a hands-on chef who manages every aspect of Il Terrazzo Carmine on a daily basis. He established the restaurant in 1984 and is especially proud that so many locals return time after time to enjoy fine dining at Il Terrazzo. The intimate dining room, which holds twenty-nine tables and has an additional five more in the bar, is set against a bright backdrop of plaid Roman shades and floral draperies. When weather permits, alfresco dining is enjoyed on a pleasant terrace with a pond and cascading waterfall. For the past twelve years, the dining experience at Il Terrazzo has been enriched by a fabulous guitarist who performs during dinner four nights a week.

Il Terrazzo's menu emphasizes Tuscan specialties such as grilled meats and venison-stuffed ravioli with wild mushroom sauce, as well as luscious traditional Italian desserts. The wine cellar has an extensive selection of wines from Italy, California, and the Northwest. Chef Carmine Esmeraldo created the following recipes for Menus and Music.

What they could my words expressed,
O my love, my all, my one!
Singing helped the verses best,
And when singing's best was done,
To my lute I left the rest.

—Robert Browning,
from "A Serenade at the Villa"

MENU

Rare Tuna with Arugula Salad
Tonno Carpaccio con Insalata di Rucola

Spaghettini with Wild Mushrooms
Spaghettini con Funghi Selvaggi

Braised Lamb Shanks
Stinco di Agnello Brasato

Pears with Gorgonzola and Caramel Sauce
Pere con Gorgonzola e Caramella

Years of practice, reflected Mrs. Fisher, chopping it up, years of actual living in Italy, would be necessary to learn the exact trick. Browning managed maccaroni wonderfully. She remembered watching him one day when he came to lunch with her father, and a dish of it had been ordered as a compliment to his connection with Italy. Fascinating, the way it went in. No chasing round the plate, no slidings off the fork, no subsequent protrusion of loose ends—just one dig, one whisk, one thrust, one gulp, and lo, yet another poet had been nourished.

—Elizabeth Von Armin, *The Enchanted April*

▪ Rare Tuna with Arugula Salad ▪

Tonno Carpaccio con Insalata di Rucola

1 tablespoon olive oil

1 pound (500 g) ahi tuna in a 3-inch-thick (7.5-cm) block

Salt and freshly ground pepper to taste

6 handfuls arugula

¼ cup (2 fl oz/60 ml) extra-virgin olive oil

1 tablespoon balsamic vinegar

In a large sauté pan or skillet over high heat, heat the olive oil and sear the tuna for about 1 minute on each side, or until lightly browned on the outside but rare on the inside. Season with salt and pepper and remove from heat. Using a very sharp large knife, cut the tuna into very thin vertical slices.

In a medium bowl, add the arugula and season with salt. Add the oil and vinegar and toss very well. Place a small mound of salad in the center of each of 6 plates and arrange a few tuna slices over the salad.

Makes 6 servings

■ Spaghettini with Wild Mushrooms ■
Spaghettini con Funghi Selvaggi

Easy to make, easy to eat.

2 tablespoons olive oil

1 pound (500 g) mushrooms (such as oysters, cremini,
  or shiitakes), sliced

2 garlic cloves, minced

1 teaspoon minced fresh rosemary

1 cup (8 fl oz/250 ml) beef broth (see Basics) or canned low-salt
  beef broth

Salt and freshly ground pepper to taste

1 pound (500 g) spaghettini

Freshly grated Parmesan cheese to taste

In a large sauté pan or skillet over high heat, heat the olive oil and sauté
the mushrooms, garlic, and rosemary until the mushrooms are browned,
about 5 minutes. Pour in the broth and cook to reduce the liquid by half.
Season with salt and pepper.

Cook the pasta in a large pot of salted boiling water until al dente,
about 8 minutes; drain. In a large serving bowl, toss the spaghettini with
the mushroom sauce. Sprinkle with cheese and serve immediately.

Makes 6 servings

■ Braised Lamb Shanks ■

Stinco di Agnello Brasato

A hearty dish that will please dinner guests on crisp autumn or blustery winter evenings. It can be made 1 or 2 days ahead and reheated.

2 tablespoons olive oil

1 large onion, chopped

2 garlic cloves, finely chopped

3 carrots, peeled and chopped

4 celery stalks, peeled and chopped

Several fresh thyme, marjoram, and rosemary sprigs, tied with kitchen string

6 lamb shanks

2 cups (16 fl oz/500 ml) dry red wine

1 tablespoon tomato paste

Salt and freshly ground pepper to taste

Preheat the oven to 400°F (200°C). In a Dutch oven or large flameproof casserole over medium heat, heat the olive oil and sauté the onion, garlic, carrot, and celery until golden brown, about 10 minutes. Add the lamb shanks and roast in the preheated oven for 20 minutes, or until lightly browned, turning frequently. Add the wine, herb bouquet, and tomato paste, and stir to scrape up any browned bits on the bottom of the pan.

Reduce the oven temperature to 350°F (180°C). Return the pan to the oven, cover, and braise for 1 hour, or until the lamb is very tender.

Using tongs, transfer the lamb shanks to a plate. Remove and discard the herbs. Place the pan or casserole over high heat, season the contents with salt and pepper, and cook to reduce to a saucelike consistency. Strain through a fine-meshed sieve, pushing the vegetables through with the back of a spoon. Arrange a lamb shank on each of 6 warmed plates and spoon some of the sauce over.

Makes 6 servings

■ Pears with Gorgonzola ■ and Caramel Sauce

Pera con Gorgonzola e Caramella

A classic combination of flavors and one of the many reasons why Gorgonzola has been made in the village of the same name since the first century A.D.; *it is now produced all over Lombardy.*

1 cup (8 oz/250 g) sugar

4 cups (32 fl oz/1 l) water

3 unpeeled firm, ripe pears

6 tablespoons (3 oz/90 g) Gorgonzola cheese at room temperature

Caramel Sauce

1 cup sugar

$\frac{1}{2}$ cup water

$\frac{1}{2}$ cup heavy (whipping) cream

In a medium saucepan, bring the sugar and water to a simmer over medium heat, stirring until the sugar dissolves. Add the pears and reduce heat to low; the liquid should remain just below a simmer. Poach the pears for 10 minutes, or until tender when pierced with a sharp knife. Remove from heat and let the pears cool in the syrup. Using a slotted spoon, carefully remove the pears. Peel, halve lengthwise, and core.

To make the caramel: In a heavy, small saucepan over high heat, combine the sugar and water and cook until golden brown. Immediately remove from heat and whisk in the cream until fully incorporated; take care, as the cream will cause the mixture to splash.

In a small bowl, cream the Gorgonzola until soft and fluffy. Stuff the hollows of the pears with the Gorgonzola. Spoon a pool of the caramel sauce onto each of 4 dessert plates and arrange a pear half in the center.

Makes 6 servings

Note: The pears can be cooked several days in advance and refrigerated in their poaching liquid.

GIACOMO CERUTI. Still Life. Pinacoteca di Brera, Milan, Italy

VA PENSIERO

Evanston, Illinois

Serving superb Northen Italian cuisine in an atmosphere reminiscent of a refined Italian country home, chef-owner Peggy Ryan lets excellent basic ingredients dictate the tastes of her earthy, robust dishes. "Women, especially in Italy, have historically cooked to please their families; they cooked to nurture. At Va Pensiero I cook to please people, in terms of portion, size, and flavor, as if they were my own family," says Ryan.

Chef Ryan's expertise in regional Italian cuisine developed largely from her ongoing commitment to learn firsthand from the great chefs of Italy—a devotion that necessitates annual trips to Italy. "I love to travel into the countryside," she says. "Each region is very specific about how it prepares a certain dish. It's great to sample a regional specialty and realize that people have been enjoying essentially the same flavors for hundreds of years." Va Pensiero (which means "thoughts depart" in Italian and is the title of an aria in Verdi's opera Nabucco) cultivates relationships with local farmers who supply the restaurant kitchen with fresh produce the morning it is picked and meat raised without hormones or chemicals. Ryan's culinary knowledge and enthusiasm for regional specialties can best be appreciated at Va Pensiero's popular monthly dinner events, during which the restaurant hosts an outstanding chef or wine maker. Diners first meet in the parlor of the historic Margarita European Inn for a brief discussion about the food and wine to come, then continue downstairs to the restaurant for a memorable six-course dinner. Chef Peggy Ryan created the following menu and recipes for Menus and Music.

MENU

Asparagus with Gorgonzola-Hazelnut Sauce

Potato Ravioli with Lobster and Shrimp Sauce

Ravioli di Patate con Aragoste e Gamberetti

Renaissance-Style Lamb Chops on Spinach
with Pine Nuts and Raisins

Costoletto di Agnello alla Rinascimento

Warm Gratin of Raspberries
with Amaretto Zabaglione

Frutti Gratinati

■ Asparagus ■
with Gorgonzola-Hazelnut Sauce

1 bunch asparagus

3 ounces (90 g) Gorgonzola or other mild blue cheese, crumbled
(about ½ cup)

Juice of 1 lemon

½ cup (4 fl oz/125 ml) heavy (whipping) cream

¼ cup (2 fl oz/60 ml) hazelnut or walnut oil

¼ cup (2 fl oz/60 ml) extra-virgin olive oil

Salt and freshly ground pepper to taste

½ cup (2 oz/60 g) hazelnuts, toasted, peeled, and coarsely chopped
(see Basics)

Snap off the ends off each asparagus spear by gently bending each stalk.
In a large pot of salted boiling water, cook the asparagus for about 4 minutes, or until crisp-tender. Drain and plunge into a bowl of ice water to
stop the cooking. Drain and pat dry with paper towels. Arrange the
asparagus on a warmed serving platter.

Combine the Gorgonzola, lemon juice, cream, nut oil, olive oil, salt,
and pepper in a jar with a tightly fitting lid. Cover and shake until well
blended. Pour the sauce over the asparagus, sprinkle with hazelnuts, and
serve immediately.

Makes 4 servings

■ Potato Ravioli ■
with Lobster and Shrimp Sauce
Ravioli di Patate con Aragoste e Gamberetti

Pasta

3½ cups (17½ oz/545 g) all-purpose flour

Pinch of salt

1 cup (8 fl oz/250 ml) dry white wine

Filling

6 large russet potatoes

¼ cup (2 fl oz/60 ml) extra-virgin olive oil

4 tablespoons (2 oz/60 g) unsalted butter

Salt and freshly ground pepper to taste

Lobster and Shrimp Sauce

One 1-pound (500 g) lobster, steamed for 7 minutes, shelled,
  cleaned, and chopped

8 ounces (250 g) shrimp, shelled and chopped

1 cup (8 oz/250 g) unsalted butter

Juice of ½ lemon

Salt and freshly ground pepper to taste

Minced fresh chives for garnish

To make the pasta: In a food processor, combine the flour, salt, and white wine and process just until a ball forms.

On a floured work surface, knead the dough until smooth and elastic, about 8 minutes. Divide the pasta into 4 balls, cover with plastic wrap, and set aside for 30 minutes before rolling out.

To make the filling: Preheat the oven to 400°F (200°C). Puncture the potatoes in a few places and bake in the preheated oven for 45 minutes, or until very tender when pierced with a knife. While the potatoes are still warm, peel and mash them until smooth. Stir in the olive oil, butter, salt and pepper.

Set the rollers of a pasta machine at the highest number. (The rollers will be wide apart.) Flatten one piece of the pasta into a rough rectangle. Feed the rectangle of pasta through the rollers. Fold in half and feed through the rollers 8 or 9 more times, folding the dough in half each time and dusting with flour if necessary to prevent sticking. Turn the dial down one notch and feed the dough through the rollers without folding. Continue to feed the dough through the rollers without folding, turning the dial one notch lower each time until the second-lowest notch is reached. The dough will be a smooth long sheet, 4 to 5 inches (10 to 13 cm) wide and about ¹/₁₆ inch (2 mm) thick. Cut the pasta sheets into 3-inch (7.5-cm) circles and place 1 tablespoon of filling in the center of half of the circles. Moisten the edges, top each circle with another pasta circle, and pinch to seal. Place the ravioli on a lightly floured tea towel, cover with another towel, and set aside until ready to cook. Repeat to roll and fill the remaining dough.

To make the sauce: In a medium bowl, combine the lobster and shrimp; set aside.

In a medium saucepan, melt the butter over medium heat and cook until browned. Remove from heat and strain the butter through a sieve lined with 2 layers of cheesecloth into a small saucepan. Stir in the lemon juice, salt, and pepper; set aside.

Cook the ravioli in a large pot of salted boiling water until they float to the top, about 3 minutes. Drain and transfer to a warmed large serving bowl. Heat the butter-lemon mixture for a minute or two and stir in the lobster-shrimp mixture. Spoon the warm sauce over the ravioli, garnish with chives, and serve immediately.

Makes 4 servings

Renaissance-Style Lamb Chops on Spinach with Pine Nuts and Raisins
Costoletto di Agnello alla Rinascimento

Marco Polo's return to Venice, which led to the opening of a direct route to the spices of the Far East and Venice's profitable spice trade monopoly, coincided with the dawn of the Renaissance.

1 tablespoon ground coriander

1 tablespoon ground cinnamon

1 tablespoon ground cumin

1 tablespoon coarsely ground pepper

1 teaspoon ground cloves

1½ teaspoons salt

12 loin lamb chops, about 1 inch (2.5 cm) thick

2 tablespoons olive oil

Spinach with Pine Nuts and Raisins (recipe follows)

Preheat the oven to 400°F (200°C). In a small bowl, stir together the spices and salt. Rub the lamb chops with the spice mixture.

In a large skillet or sauté pan over high heat, heat the olive oil and brown the lamb chops in batches for 1 or 2 minutes on each side; they will still be very rare in the center. Transfer the lamb chops to a roasting pan and roast in the preheated oven for about 7 minutes for medium rare.

Arrange the spinach in a nest in the center of a large warmed platter. Drain off any excess liquid and encircle the spinach with the lamb chops. Or, serve 2 lamb chops and a mound of spinach on each of 6 warmed plates. Serve immediately.

Makes 6 servings

Spinach with Pine Nuts and Raisins

2 tablespoons olive oil

3 bunches spinach, stemmed

½ cup (3 oz/90 g) golden raisins, soaked in warm water
   for 10 minutes and drained

¼ cup (1 oz/30 g) pine nuts

Salt and freshly ground pepper to taste

In a large skillet or sauté pan over medium heat, heat the olive oil and
sauté all the ingredients until the spinach is just wilted, turning often with
tongs. Remove from heat and drain; do not squeeze. Serve immediately.

Makes 6 servings

■ Warm Gratin of Raspberries ■ with Amaretto Zabaglione

Frutti Gratinati

Fresh raspberries covered with a heavenly almond-flavored foam.

8 cups (2 lb/1 kg) fresh raspberries

Zabaglione

6 egg yolks

½ cup (4 oz/125 g) sugar

½ cup (4 fl oz/125 ml) vin santo* or other white dessert wine

¼ cup (2 fl oz/60 ml) amaretto**

Preheat the broiler. Arrange the raspberries evenly in a 10-inch (25-cm) gratin dish or quiche pan.

To make the zabaglione: In the top half of a double boiler, whisk the eggs and sugar together until pale, about 2 minutes. Place over barely simmering water and gradually whisk in the wine and amaretto. Continue beating until thickened and doubled in volume.

Spoon the zabaglione over the raspberries. Broil under the preheated broiler, 5 inches (13 cm) from the heat source, for 1 to 2 minutes, or until the top is dappled with brown. Serve immediately.

Makes 6 to 8 servings

*Vin santo, or "holy wine," is produced in Tuscany from semi-dried grapes with a long, slow fermentation followed by many years of aging. The result is an intensely flavored, sweet golden wine.

**Amaretto is a sweet liqueur flavored with almonds or the kernels from apricot pits.

CARAVAGGIO. Young Bacchus. Uffizi, Florence, Italy

Let me purify my mouth
In a holy cup o' th' South;
In a golden pitcher let me
Head and ears for comfort get me,
And drink of the wine of the vine benign
That sparkles warm in Sansovine.

—Francesco Redi,
from "Bacchus on Beverages"

VALENTINO

Santa Monica, California

Born in Sicily, Piero Selvaggio arrived in Los Angeles as an eighteen-year-old with dreams of making a name for himself. As a university student studying Romance languages, he took a job as busboy in his uncle's restaurant, and in 1972, at age twenty-four, he opened Valentino with a friend. At first, the restaurant served "Continental" food, offering dishes such as veal piccata and fettuccine Alfredo. But Valentino evolved over the decades, and Selvaggio gradually introduced his customers to authentic Italian foods such as porcini, white truffles, extra-virgin olive oils, Parmigiano-Reggiano, mozzarella di bufala, and prosciutto. As one of the leaders in the movement to bring Italian cooking back to its roots, Selvaggio has helped transform Americans' ideas of what Italian cooking is all about.

Today, Valentino is one of the finest restaurants in the United States, and enjoying contemporary Italian cuisine here is a grand experience. A master is at work in the kitchen, the service is exceptionally gracious, the wine list is extraordinary, and the dining room decor is sleek and sophisticated. Chef Angelo Auriana's cooking celebrates unusually fine ingredients as well as artisan-crafted food products. A native of Bergamo, Auriana's cooking style is innovative yet faithful to regional Italian culinary traditions, and his dishes fairly sing when paired with Selvaggio's wine choices. Probably the best way to discover what Valentino has to offer is to let Selvaggio orchestrate the menu and the wines to go with it. Passionate about wine, Selvaggio has amassed one of the world's great wine cellars, and since 1981 it has received the *Wine Spectator's* Grand Award. Every stellar wine is represented on the list, with over 1,300 choices. Italian producers have such respect and affection for Selvaggio that when he lost 30,000 bottles in the Northridge earthquake of 1994, they rallied to send cases of rare, old, and hard-to-find wines to replace what he had lost. Chef Angelo Auriana presented *Menus and Music* with the following menu and recipes.

MENU

Sea Scallops
with Cannellini Beans and Bottarga

Porcini-Infused Gnocchi
with Truffled Fonduta Sauce

Roasted Baby Lamb Chops
in Balsamic Vinegar
with Asparagus

Orange Semifreddo

■ Sea Scallops ■
with Cannellini Beans and Bottarga

2 tablespoons extra-virgin olive oil, plus more for drizzling

12 sea scallops

Salt and freshly ground pepper to taste

3 cups (21 oz/655 g) cooked cannellini beans, heated

Grated bottarga (dried tuna roe)* or caviar to taste for serving

In a large sauté pan or skillet over high heat, heat the 2 tablespoons olive oil and sear the scallops for 2 minutes on each side, or until lightly browned on the outside and opaque throughout. Season with salt and pepper; set aside and keep warm.

Place a mound of cannellini beans in the center of each of 6 warmed plates. Arrange 2 scallops on top of each mound of beans and top with grated bottarga or caviar. Drizzle with olive oil and serve immediately.

Makes 6 servings

*Bottarga, the dried, pressed roe of mullet or tuna, comes mostly from Sardinia and Sicily. Sold and eaten throughout Italy, it is regarded as a great delicacy and is very expensive. Bottarga is available at some Italian foods stores (see Resources). Covered with plastic wrap, it will keep for several months.

Porcini-Infused Gnocchi ■ with Truffled Fonduta

Potato gnocchi, a Piedmontese specialty made with potatoes, eggs, and a little flour, are traditionally served with a sauce made by melting Fontina cheese with cream. The gnocchi may be kept in a self-sealing plastic bag in the refrigerator for 2 to 3 days before cooking.

Gnocchi

3 ounces (90 g) dried porcini

4 unpeeled russet potatoes (about 2 lb/1 kg)

2 cups (10 oz/315 g) all-purpose flour, plus more if needed

2 eggs

1 cup (4 oz/125 g) freshly grated Parmesan cheese

1 teaspoon salt

Freshly ground pepper to taste

Fonduta Sauce

1 cup (8 fl oz/250 ml) heavy (whipping) cream

5 ounces (155 g) shredded Fontina or Gruyère cheese

White truffle oil for drizzling*

Soak the porcini in warm water to cover for 30 minutes; drain, reserving the soaking liquid.

Meanwhile, cook the potatoes in a large pot of salted boiling water until very tender, 30 to 40 minutes; drain and peel while still hot. In a large bowl, mash the potatoes just to break them up; do not overmash or they will become glutinous.

In a blender or food processor, purée the porcini to a thick paste, adding a little of the soaking liquid if necessary.

Spread the flour on a pastry board. Mound the potatoes on top. Make a well in the center and add the eggs, porcini purée, cheese, salt, and pepper. Using a fork, beat the eggs with the purée and cheese just until blended. Gradually mix in the flour to make a smooth, slightly sticky dough, adding more flour 1 tablespoon at a time if necessary.

Divide the dough into 8 portions. On the floured board, use your hands to roll each portion into a long rope about 1 inch (2.5 cm) in diameter. Placing the ropes so they are side by side, use a floured knife to cut each crosswise into 1-inch (2.5-cm) cylinders.

In a large pot of salted boiling water, cook the gnocchi until they float to the top. Using a slotted spoon, transfer them to a warmed bowl.

To make the fonduta: In a double boiler over barely simmering water, combine the cream and cheese and stir constantly until the cheese melts and the mixture is creamy; do not let boil.

Pour the fonduta over the gnocchi, toss lightly, and divide among 6 warmed shallow bowls. Drizzle each serving with a little truffle oil and serve at once.

Makes 6 servings

*White truffle oil is available at Italian markets and specialty foods stores (see Resources).

■ Roasted Baby Lamb Chops ■
in Balsamic Vinegar with Asparagus

In this dish, garlic, balsamic vinegar, and fresh herbs infuse lamb chops with delicious results. At Valentino, the dish is served with white asparagus when it is in season. Green asparagus makes a fine substitute.

2 racks of lamb, trimmed of fat

2 garlic cloves

Balsamic vinegar for sprinkling

1 tablespoon mixed minced fresh mint, sage, and rosemary

Salt and freshly ground pepper to taste

1 bunch jumbo white or green asparagus, trimmed

3 tablespoons chicken broth (see Basics) or canned low-salt chicken broth

Rub the lamb with the garlic cloves. Arrange the lamb in a roasting pan and sprinkle with the balsamic vinegar and herbs. Cover and refrigerate for 2 to 4 hours.

Preheat the oven to 350°F (180°C). Season the lamb with salt and pepper and bake in the preheated oven for 20 minutes for medium rare; set aside.

Meanwhile, peel each asparagus stalk from the tip to the bottom. Cook the asparagus in a covered steamer over rapidly simmering water until crisp-tender, 3 to 4 minutes.

Cut the lamb into 18 chops, reserving the juices. Arrange the chops and steamed asparagus on a warmed serving platter or 6 warmed plates.

Pour off the fat from the roasting pan. Add the reserved lamb juices and the broth and boil until reduced to a saucelike consistency. Drizzle the sauce over the lamb chops and asparagus and serve at once.

Makes 6 servings

■ Orange Semifreddo ■

Semifreddo literally means "half cold" and refers to a variety of soft frozen desserts, including rich gelatos like this one. You don't need an ice cream maker to make this semifreddo. At Valentino, it is served in thick slices and drizzled with strawberry compote and orange sauce.

1¾ cups (14 fl oz/430 ml) fresh orange juice

¼ cup (2 fl oz/60 ml) fresh lemon juice

½ cup (4 fl oz/125 ml) limoncello*

1½ cups (12 fl oz/375 ml) heavy (whipping) cream

¼ cup (2 fl oz/60 ml) Grand Marnier or other orange liqueur

½ cup (4 oz/125 g) sugar

Julienned zest of 2 oranges

4 egg yolks

2 eggs

Chill a 6-cup loaf pan in the freezer for 30 minutes. Line the pan with long pieces of plastic wrap, letting the ends hang over the sides.

In a small, heavy saucepan, boil the orange juice, lemon juice, and limoncello over medium-high heat until reduced to a syrupy consistency.

In a deep bowl, beat the cream and Grand Marnier together until soft peaks form. Cover and refrigerate.

In a food processor, combine the sugar, orange zest, egg yolks, and eggs until the zest is finely chopped. Transfer to a double boiler over barely simmering water and stir constantly until very thick, about 10 minutes. (Don't let this get too got, or the eggs can scramble.) Set the top of the double boiler in a bowl of ice cubes and whisk until cool.

Stir in the orange juice mixture and gently fold in the whipped cream. Pour into the prepared pan, cover with the ends of the plastic wrap, and freeze for at least 8 hours or overnight.

Just before serving, invert the semifreddo and unmold. Using a knife dipped in warm water, cut into ¾-inch (2-cm) slices.

Makes 8 servings

*Limoncello is a sweet liqueur made from the peel of the lemons that grow in profusion and to an extraordinary size on the Amalfi Coast.

CRISTOFORO MUNARI. Still Life. Uffizi, Florence, Italy

HOTEL VILLA CIPRIANI

Asolo, Italy

Situated in the gentle rolling hills of Asolo, Hotel Villa Cipriani is surrounded by a lovely garden overlooking the Veneto countryside, a source of artistic inspiration for the likes of Titian, Giorgione, Palladio, and Robert Browning, who wrote while living in the villa: "Open my heart and you will see / Graved inside of it, 'Italy'."

Built in the Palladian era by an unknown architect, the villa was once the home of English poets Elizabeth and Robert Browning. In the 1950s, the property was acquired by the Guinness family, who maintained it as a country inn. In 1962, the Guinnesses passed the management to Giuseppe Cipriani, the founder of Harry's Bar in Venice. Today, the villa is a charming hotel, having been transformed by the Cipriani family with care to preserve its ancient charms. Opening off cool corridors of polished stone, the luxurious guest rooms have enchanting views, beamed ceilings, and lovely antiques. Guests enjoy Villa Cipriani's outstanding service and emphasis on creative cuisine and fine wines.

Near Asolo can be found some of the most famous villas designed by Andrea Palladio, and to this day the area is favored by artists and intellectuals. Ciosue' Darducci called Asolo "the city with a thousand landscapes," and Eleanora Duse, the famous actress of the early 1900s, lived in Asolo and is buried there. An annual international music festival is held here in September, and a vast antique market takes place every second weekend of each month, except July and August.

Ristorante Villa Cipriani offers chef Secondo Ceccato's superb seasonal menu, including such traditional Veneto fare as risotto all'asolana and Venetian-style liver and onions, as well as shrimp, sea bass, and lobster purchased daily from the Chioggia market. In spring and summer, dishes are built around white asparagus from Bassano, baby goat and lamb, organic peas from Borso del Grappa, and zucchini blossoms. Porcini and chiodini mushrooms, white truffles, and radicchio from Treviso are highlights in autumn and winter. During warm weather, alfresco lunches and romantic candlelight dinners are enjoyed in the lovely garden.

           . . . earth,
         sky,
    Hill, vale, tree, flower,—Italia's rare
       O'er running beauty crowds the eye—
        — Robert Browning, from "Asolando"

HOTEL VILLA CIPRIANI

MENU

Fresh Salmon Tartare
Salmone Fresco Tartare

Pasta and Bean Soup
Pasta e Fagioli

Pasta with Shrimp, Tomatoes, and Basil
Pappardelle con Scampi, Pomodoro, e Basilico

Calf's Liver, Venetian Style
Fegato di Vitello alla Veneziana

Tiramisù
Tiramisù

■ Fresh Salmon Tartare ■

Salmone Fresco Tartare

Elegant and easy to make, this appetizer combines both fresh and smoked salmon and is served on crostini.

3 ounces (90 g) smoked salmon, finely diced

10 ounces (315 g) salmon fillet, skinned and finely diced

Juice of 1 lemon

Salt and freshly ground pepper to taste

1 small leek (white part only), finely diced

2 tablespoons extra-virgin olive oil

2 tablespoons Cognac or brandy

Capers for garnish, drained

Crostini (see Basics)

In a medium bowl, stir the smoked salmon, salmon fillet, lemon juice, salt, and pepper together. Add the leek, olive oil, and Cognac or brandy and stir until blended. Spoon the salmon mixture onto the crostini and garnish each with a caper.

Makes 6 servings

HOTEL VILLA CIPRIANI

■ Calf's Liver, Venetian Style ■
Fegato di Vitello alla Veneziana

In this famous dish, the liver is cooked very briefly over high heat. The onions, on the other hand, are cooked very slowly over low heat to produce a sweet flavor. Serve with grilled polenta, the rustic cornmeal dish that for centuries has been a staple food of the Veneto region.

2 tablespoons butter

2 tablespoons olive oil

2 red onions, thinly sliced

1 pound (500 g) calf's liver, cut into 1½-by-¼-inch (4-by-½-cm) strips

Salt and freshly ground pepper to taste

⅓ cup (3 fl oz/80 ml) dry white wine

Minced fresh flat-leaf parsley for garnish

In a large sauté pan or skillet, melt the butter with the olive oil over medium-low heat. Cook the onions, stirring frequently, for 15 to 20 minutes, or until soft and golden. Using a slotted spoon, transfer the onions to a plate. Increase heat to high and sauté the liver for 30 seconds on each side, or until lightly browned. Season with salt and pepper. Return the onions to the pan, add the wine, and stir for 1 minute. Divide the liver and onions among 4 warmed plates, garnish with parsley, and serve immediately.

Makes 4 servings

■ Pasta ■
with Shrimp, Tomatoes, and Basil

Pappardelle con Scampi, Pomodoro, e Basilico

Scampi, crustaceans similar to crayfish, are not readily available in U.S. markets. Use shrimp instead. Dried pappardelle or fettuccine may be substituted for the fresh pasta.

3 tablespoons olive oil

1 large garlic clove, crushed

1 pound (500 g) medium shrimp, shelled and deveined

2 tablespoons Cognac or brandy

1½ cups (12 oz/375 g) canned peeled whole tomatoes with juice, chopped

Salt and freshly ground pepper to taste

12 ounces (375 g) fresh Whole-Wheat Pappardelle (recipe follows)

⅓ cup (½ oz/15 g) fresh basil leaves, chopped, plus basil sprigs for garnish

¼ cup (⅓ oz/10 g) fresh flat-leaf parsley leaves, chopped

In a large, heavy sauté pan or skillet over medium heat, heat the olive oil and sauté the garlic for 2 minutes, or until barely golden; discard the garlic. Increase heat to medium high and sauté the shrimp for 1 minute. Add the Cognac or brandy and carefully ignite with a long-handled match. When the flames subside, add the tomatoes and their juice, the salt, and pepper. Simmer just until the shrimp are pink and firm, about 3 minutes; remove from heat.

In a large pot of salted boiling water, cook the pappardelle for 2 to 3 minutes, or until al dente; drain. Add the pasta, chopped basil, and parsley to the shrimp mixture over medium-high heat and toss until heated through. Transfer to a warmed large pasta bowl or 4 individual pasta bowls. Garnish with basil sprigs and serve immediatcly.

Makes 4 servings

■ Whole-Wheat Pappardelle ■

The broadest of the fresh ribbon pastas.

1¼ cups (6½ oz/220 g) all-purpose flour

½ cup (2½ oz/75 g) whole-wheat flour

½ teaspoon salt

2 eggs

2 egg yolks

1 tablespoon extra-virgin olive oil

1 to 3 teaspoons water

In a medium bowl, stir together the all-purpose flour, whole-wheat flour, and salt. Pour the flour mixture into a mound on a work surface and make a well in the center. Add the eggs, egg yolks, olive oil, and 1 teaspoon of the water to the well. Using a fork, beat the eggs, yolks, and liquid ingredients until blended. Begin mixing the flour into the egg mixture, drawing the flour from the inside wall of the well until a dough is formed. Alternatively, combine the ingredients in a food processor and process just until a ball forms. On a floured work surface, knead the dough until smooth and elastic, about 8 minutes. Cover with plastic wrap and let rest for 30 minutes before rolling out.

Set the rollers of a pasta machine at the highest number. Flatten one piece into a rough rectangle and feed it through the rollers. Fold the rectangle in half and feed through the rollers 8 or 9 more times, folding the dough in half each time and dusting it with flour if necessary to prevent sticking. Turn the dial down one notch and feed the dough through the rollers without folding. Continue feeding the dough through the rollers without folding, turning the dial one notch lower each time until the second-lowest notch is reached. The dough will be a long, smooth sheet, 4 to 5 inches (10 cm to 13 cm) wide. Dust the dough on both sides with flour and fold crosswise in half 2 or 3 times; do not press together. Roll the remaining dough in same manner.

With a fluted pastry wheel, cut the folded dough lengthwise into 1-inch-wide (2.5-cm) noodles. Unfold the pasta and cut the noodles into 6-inch (15-cm) lengths. Toss the pappardelle with a little flour to separate the strands and prevent sticking.

Makes 12 ounces (375 g) pappardelle

■ Pasta and Bean Soup ■

Pasta e Fagioli

A hearty, comforting soup thickened with mashed beans. Start this recipe the day before you plan to serve it, as the soup tastes best the day after it's made.

2 cups (14 oz/440 g) dried borlotti* or Great Northern beans, soaked overnight in water to cover by 2 inches (5 cm)

5 bacon slices, chopped

1 onion, chopped

1 garlic clove, minced

9 cups (72 fl oz/2.1 l) water

½ cup (3½ oz/105 g) ditalini (short tubular pasta) or subiotini (small flat pasta squares) or other small dried pasta shapes

Salt to taste

Extra-virgin olive oil and freshly ground pepper for garnish

Drain the beans. In a large, heavy pot, sauté the bacon, onion, and garlic over medium heat for 7 minutes, or until the onion is translucent. Increase heat to high, add the beans, and pour in the water. Bring the soup to a boil, reduce heat to low, cover, and simmer very slowly for 4 hours, or until the beans are tender.

Using a slotted spoon, transfer 3 cups (21 oz/655 g) beans to a medium bowl and reserve. Stir the pasta into the soup. Cover and simmer for 9 minutes, or until the pasta is al dente. Using a fork, mash the reserved beans in the bowl, or transfer the beans to a blender or food processor and pulse briefly. Stir the mashed beans into the soup and season generously with salt.

Ladle the soup into bowls, drizzle with olive oil, and add a grind of pepper.

Makes 6 servings

*Red and cream speckled borlotti beans are also called cranberry or cargamento beans. Available at Italian and specialty foods shops and by mail (see Resources).

■ Tiramisù ■

Tiramisù

A luscious combination of mascarpone (Italian cream cheese), ladyfingers, and coffee in a rich cocoa-dusted dessert.

5 egg yolks

5 tablespoons (3 oz/90 g) sugar

1 cup (8 oz/250 g) mascarpone cheese* at room temperature

3 egg whites

⅓ cup (3 fl oz/80 ml) heavy cream, whipped

1 tablespoon dark rum, or to taste

1 tablespoon fresh lemon juice

1 teaspoon vanilla extract

16 ladyfingers (savoiardi), see Basics

¼ cup (2 fl oz/60 ml) freshly brewed espresso coffee

Unsweetened cocoa powder for dusting

Beat the egg yolks and 3 tablespoons of the sugar until pale in color. Add the rum and beat until well blended. Mix in the mascarpone until smooth and light; do not overbeat or the mixture may separate.

In a large bowl, beat the egg whites with the remaining 2 tablespoons sugar until stiff, glossy peaks form. In a deep bowl, beat the cream until stiff peaks form. Fold in the whipped cream, lemon juice, and vanilla. Fold the egg white mixture into the mascarpone mixture.

In a shallow bowl, add the coffee and briefly dip 8 ladyfingers into the coffee on each side. Arrange in a single layer in a 9-inch-diameter (23-cm) bowl. Cover the ladyfingers with half the mascarpone mixture. Repeat with the remaining ladyfingers and mascarpone mixture. Dust the top with cocoa powder and refrigerate for at least 4 hours or overnight before serving.

Makes 4 to 6 servings

*Mascarpone, a delicately flavored triple-cream cheese from Lombardy, is usually sold in plastic containers in many grocery stores and most Italian foods stores.

Note: If you are concerned about eating uncooked eggs, do not make this recipe.

HOTEL VILLA CIPRIANI

GIOVANNA GARZONI. A Dish of Small Pears with Medlars and Cherries. Galleria Palatina, Palazzo Pitti, Florence, Italy

VILLA DEL LUPO

Vancouver, British Columbia

Villa del Lupo provides a sensual experience for food lovers. Diners enjoy superb regional Italian cuisine, an extensive wine selection, cozy candlelit tables, contemporary art, and personalized service in a turn-of-the-century historic home in the heart of downtown Vancouver. The restaurant is owned and managed by Julio Gonzalez-Perini and Chris Riley, who together have created what many people consider the best Italian restaurant in Vancouver. The menu includes market-fresh daily specials, as well as three fixed-price menus that feature local organic ingredients. Highlights include grilled antipasti, handmade fresh pastas, lamb osso buco, delectable vegetarian dishes, and luscious traditional Italian desserts.

Villa del Lupo's lovely, intimate dining spaces include an upstairs room with its own full-service bar and the living room, which is warmed by a working fireplace. Music softens the mood in the romantic wine-cellar dining room, where up to six guests can dine in an atmosphere reminiscent of a Tuscan winery. Chef Julio Gonzalez-Perini created the following menu and recipes for Menus and Music.

MENU

Porcini Mushroom Soufflé

Sea Bass Fillets with Fennel Purée

Caramelized Pears with Honey Ice Cream
and Chocolate Sauce

The house for me, no doubt, were a house in the city-square;
Ah, such a life, such a life, as one leads at the window there!
Something to see, by Bacchus, something to hear, at least!
There, the whole day long, one's life is a perfect feast

—Robert Browning,
from "Up in the Villa-Down in the City"

■ Porcini Mushroom Soufflé ■

½ ounce (15 g) dried porcini mushrooms

½ cup (4 fl oz/125 ml) warm water

½ tablespoon dry Marsala wine*

½ cup (2 oz/60 g) freshly grated Parmesan cheese

2 egg yolks

1 tablespoon butter, melted, plus 1 tablespoon butter

½ teaspoon salt

¼ teaspoon freshly ground pepper

½ cup (4 fl oz/125 ml) milk

2½ tablespoons flour

1 cup (8 fl oz/250 ml) heavy (whipping) cream

1 large egg white

Preheat the oven to 375°F (190°C). Butter four 1-cup (8-fl oz/250-ml) ramekins or ovenproof cups. Line the bottom of each ramekin or cup with parchment paper and butter well.

In a small bowl, combine the porcini and water; soak for 30 minutes. Drain the porcini, reserving the soaking liquid. Rinse the porcini, pat dry with paper towels, and coarsely chop. In a small bowl, combine the porcini with the Marsala, ⅓ cup of the Parmesan cheese, the egg yolks, the melted butter, salt, and pepper.

In a small saucepan, heat the milk over medium heat until bubbles form around the edges. Whisk in the flour until smooth and thick. Stir in the chopped porcini and cream.

In a large bowl, beat the egg white until stiff peaks form. Fold the egg white into the porcini mixture.

Fill each ramekin or cup half full with the soufflé mixture. Place in a large baking pan. Add enough hot water to reach halfway up the sides of the ramekins or cups. Bake in the preheated oven for 20 minutes, or until the soufflés are puffed and golden brown.

Remove from the oven and let the soufflés rest. Run a small knife around the edge of each soufflé and invert onto a plate.

Meanwhile, to make the sauce: Pour all but the last half inch (12 mm) of the mushroom soaking liquid into a small saucepan. Boil over high heat until reduced by half. Reduce heat to medium and swirl in the remaining 1 tablespoon butter until melted. Stir in the remaining 3 tablespoons Parmesan cheese.

Drizzle the sauce over each soufflé and serve at once.

Makes 4 servings

*Marsala, a rich fortified wine that is available either sweet or dry, is produced near the city of Marsala, in Sicily.

■ Sea Bass Fillets with Fennel Purée ■

The fresh flavors of fennel, lime, and dill spark this light, quickly made dish.

1 large fennel bulb (about 8 oz/250 g), trimmed and coarsely
   chopped

1 carrot, peeled and coarsely chopped

2 teaspoons minced fresh cilantro leaves

10 tablespoons (9 fl oz/280 ml) extra-virgin olive oil

Salt and freshly ground pepper to taste

1 tomato, peeled, seeded, and chopped (see Basics)

Juice of 1 lime

Minced fresh dill to taste

Salt and freshly ground pepper to taste

½ cup (4 fl oz/125 ml) extra virgin olive oil

4 Chilean sea bass fillets (about 2 lb/1 kg)

4 fresh dill sprigs for garnish

To make the fennel purée: Steam the fennel and carrot in a covered steamer over rapidly simmering water for 30 minutes, or until tender. Remove from heat and transfer to a food processor. Add the cilantro and purée. Stir in 2 tablespoons of the olive oil; set aside and keep warm.

In a medium bowl, whisk together 6 tablespoons (3 fl oz/90 ml) of the olive oil, the tomato, lime juice, dill, salt, and pepper until emulsified; set aside.

In a large sauté pan or skillet over medium-high heat, heat the remaining 2 tablespoons olive oil and add the sea bass fillets, skin-side down. Cook on each side until browned on the outside and opaque throughout.

To serve, pour a little of the olive oil mixture onto each of 4 warmed plates. Place a seabass fillet, skin-side up, on each plate. Add an oval-shaped scoop of the fennel purée to each plate, garnish with dill, and serve immediately.

Makes 4 servings

VILLA DEL LUPO

■ Caramelized Pears ■ with Honey Ice Cream and Chocolate Sauce

Honey Ice Cream

¼ cup (3 oz/90 g) flavorful honey

4 egg yolks

1 cup (8 fl oz/250 ml) milk, heated

⅔ cup (5 oz/150 ml) half-and-half

1 cup (8 fl oz/250 ml) water

¼ cup (2 oz/60 g) sugar

1 vanilla bean, split lengthwise, or 1 teaspoon vanilla extract

Juice of 1 lemon

2 large pears, peeled, halved, and cored

Chocolate Sauce

5 ounces (155 g) semisweet chocolate, coarsely chopped

1 tablespoon unsalted butter

Sugar for sprinkling

4 fresh mint sprigs for garnish

To make the ice cream: Heat the honey in a double boiler over barely simmering water. Add the egg yolks and whisk until the mixture doubles in volume. Gradually stir in the hot milk and cook, stirring constantly, until the mixture thickens enough to coat the spoon, about 5 minutes. Strain through a fine-meshed sieve into a bowl. Stir in the half-and-half. Let cool to room temperature. Cover and refrigerate until chilled, about 2 hours. Freeze in an ice cream maker according to the manufacturer's instructions.

To make the chocolate sauce: In a double boiler over barely simmering water, melt the chocolate. Swirl in the butter until smooth and creamy. Set aside and keep warm.

In a saucepan over medium heat, bring the water, ¼ cup (2 oz/60 g) sugar, vanilla bean, if using, and lemon juice to a simmer. Add the pears and cook just below a simmer for 5 to 8 minutes, or until the pears are soft when pierced with a knife; actual simmering may burst the fruit. Set the pears aside to cool in the liquid.

Preheat a broiler. Cut the pears into thin slices and fan them out onto each of 4 serving plates. Sprinkle the pears with sugar and broil about 2 inches from the heat source until the sugar caramelizes, 30 seconds to 1 minute; watch carefully so the sugar doesn't burn. Pour the chocolate sauce around the pear slices and add 2 small scoops of honey ice cream. Garnish with mint and serve immediately.

Makes 4 servings

Madrigal 109

Ravished by all that to the eyes is fair
Yet hungry for the joys that truly bless,
My soul can find no stair
To mount to heaven, save earth's loveliness.

Madrigale 109

Gli occhi mie', vaghi delle cose belle,
E l'alma insieme della sua salute
Non anno altra virtute
C' ascende a ciel che mirar tutte quelle.
—Michelangelo Buonarroti

VILLA SAN MICHELE

Fiesole, Italy

Designated as a monument by Italy's National Trust and surrounded by a protected forest of cypress, cedars, and olives, Villa San Michele nestles in the hills of Fiesole overlooking the city of Florence. Its magnificent colonnaded façade was designed by none other than Michelangelo, and the building is located near the hill where Leonardo da Vinci experimented with flying.

Today, Villa San Michele offers an experience imbued with history, as well as a singularly comforting combination of Franciscan simplicity and well-thought-out luxury. Hotel guests enjoy the villa's magnificent frescoes, arcades, patios, antiques, and tranquil terraced gardens. Formerly a fifteenth-century monastery, the hotel lobby was once a chapel, and many of the well-appointed guest rooms were the cells of monks. A lavish breakfast buffet is arrayed beneath a brilliant Arazzo tapestry: moist cakes of raisins and candied fruits; farmhouse eggs; seasonal fruits; fresh pecorino and aged Parmigiano-Reggiano cheeses; platters of local salami, Parma ham, and prosciutto; fruit tarts; fresh-squeezed fruit juices; and espresso. Thus fortified, most guests choose to catch the regularly scheduled shuttle service to the center of Florence, while some prefer to spend the day within the rare sanctuary of the villa, surrendering their senses to its art, serene gardens, luxurious luncheon menu, and swimming pool with a small mountain-spring waterfall. Visits can be arranged to Chianti, the Medici villas, San Gimignano, Siena, and the Tuscan countryside. Special cooking classes are offered at Villa San Michele several times a year.

In the evening, dinner is served in the elegant Cenacolo Restaurant, with its fine paintings, tapestries, and huge stone fireplace, or alfresco in the more informal setting of the Loggia restaurant, with its magnificent views of Florence and the Arno valley. A resident pianist performs most evenings, and Vittorio Dall'Ò, the personable and knowledgeable restaurant manager, will assist you with the superb seasonal Tuscan menu and celebrated wine list. Highlights of chef Attilio Fabrizio's menu include delicate housemade pasta, wild mushrooms, game, and meats; the desserts are delectable works of art. The loggia leads through to an enchanting garden, where diners may linger after dinner and enjoy the perfumed air of the citrus garden. The following recipes were presented to Menus and Music by master chef Attilio di Fabrizio.

> . . . no dumb thunder rolled
> In the valley beneath where, white and wide
> And washed by the morning water-gold,
> Florence lay out on the mountain-side.
>
> River and bridge and street and square
> Lay mine, as much at my beck and call,
> Through the live translucent bath of air,
> As the sights in a magic crystal ball.
>
> —Robert Browning,
> from "Old Pictures in Florence"

MENU

Eggplant and Goat Cheese Tortelloni with Thyme Sauce

Tortelloni di Melanzane e Caprino con Salsa al Timo

Red Mullet Salad

Insalata di Triglie di Scoglio

Baked Rack of Lamb with Bread Crumbs and Herbs

Carrè d'Agnello Gratinato alle Erbe

Orange Cream-Filled Charlottes

Piccola Charlotte all'Aurum

Now it is all dark. Now Beauty and Passion seem never to have existed. I know. But remember the mountains over Florence and the view.

—E. M. Forster, *A Room with a View*

▪ Eggplant and Goat Cheese Tortelloni ▪ with Thyme Sauce

Tortelloni di Melanzane e Caprino con Salsa al Timo

At Villa San Michele, these tortelloni are filled with caprino, little disc-shaped goat cheeses. Fresh caprino doesn't travel well and is rarely found outside Italy, but it is widely available bottled in olive oil flavored with herbs and chilies. Drain before using. Tortelloni are larger than tortellini; these are formed in the shape of half-moons. Sheets of commercial fresh pasta may be substituted for the homemade pasta.

Filling

2 eggplants (1 lb/500 g), peeled and diced

1½ tablespoons salt

2 tablespoons olive oil

½ garlic clove, minced

Leaves from 2 fresh thyme sprigs, chopped

½ cup (4 fl oz/125 ml) beef broth (see Basics) or canned beef broth

5 ounces (155 g) caprino or fresh white goat cheese

Thyme Sauce

3 tablespoons unsalted butter

½ cup (⅔ oz/20 g) minced fresh thyme

1⅔ cups (13 fl oz/405 ml) heavy (whipping) cream

⅓ cup (1½ oz/45 g) freshly grated Parmesan cheese

Pasta

2½ cups (12½ oz/390 g) all-purpose flour

4 eggs

Pinch of salt

Place the eggplant on a plate and sprinkle with the salt. Place another plate on top and top with a weight, such as a heavy skillet or cans of food. Let drain for 2 hours. Rinse and pat the eggplant dry with paper towels.

In a large sauté pan or skillet over medium heat, heat the olive oil and sauté the eggplant, garlic, and thyme for 2 to 3 minutes. Add the broth and simmer until the liquid evaporates and the eggplant is soft, about 15 minutes. Set aside and let cool. In a blender or food processor, combine the eggplant mixture and goat cheese; process until smooth.

To make the sauce: In a large saucepan, melt the butter over medium heat with the thyme until the butter begins to brown. Pour in the cream and simmer for about 5 minutes. Add the Parmesan cheese and simmer for 3 to 4 minutes.

To make the pasta: Pour the flour into a mound on a work surface and make a well in the center. Add the eggs and salt to the well, and using a fork, beat just until blended. Begin mixing the flour into the egg mixture, drawing the flour from the inside wall of the well until a dough is formed. Alternatively, add the flour, eggs, and salt to the bowl of a food processor and process just until a ball forms.

On a lightly floured work surface, knead the dough until smooth and elastic, about 8 minutes. Cover with plastic wrap and let rest for at least 30 minutes before rolling out.

Set the rollers of a pasta machine at the highest number. Flatten one piece of dough into a rough rectangle and feed it through the rollers. Fold in half and feed through the rollers 8 or 9 more times, folding the dough in half each time and dusting with flour if necessary to prevent sticking. Turn the dial down one notch and feed through the rollers without folding. Continue to feed the dough through the rollers without folding, turning the dial one notch lower each time until the second-lowest notch is reached. The dough will be a long, smooth sheet, 4 to 5 inches (10 cm to 13 cm) wide.

Cut the pasta into thirty-six 4-inch (10-cm) rounds. Place about 2 tablespoons of the filling in the center of each round. Moisten the edges with a little water and fold the pasta over, forming a half-moon. Press the edges together to close well. Repeat to roll, fill, and shape the remaining dough.

In a large pot of salted boiling water, cook the tortelloni until they float to the top, about 3 minutes.

Gently drain the tortelloni and transfer them to the pan with the thyme sauce. Toss gently to coat with sauce. Serve immediately.

Makes 6 servings

■ Red Mullet Salad ■

Insalata di Triglie di Scoglio

As delicious as it is beautiful! The different elements of this dish are assembled in the shape of a butterfly. The recipe calls for the tiny red mullets of the Mediterranean; if small ones are unavailable, use larger ones, sometimes sold as "goatfish," and cut the fillets into strips. Red trout or sole fillets may be substituted.

18 carrot slices

18 zucchini slices

12 small red mullets, red trout, or sole fillets

Salt to taste

Flour for dredging

2 tablespoons olive oil

10 handfuls mixed salad greens

¼ cup (2 fl oz/60 ml) walnut oil

12 fresh chives, about 3 inches (8 cm) long

In separate saucepans of salted boiling water, cook the carrots and zucchini for 2 or 3 minutes, or until crisp-tender.

Season the fish fillets with salt and dredge lightly in flour. In a large sauté pan or skillet over medium-high heat, heat the olive oil and sauté the fish for 1 or 2 minutes on each side, or until golden brown and crisp.

In a large bowl, toss the salad greens with the walnut oil. Arrange a bed of greens on each of 6 dishes. Arrange a row of 3 carrot slices alternating with 3 zucchini slices over the salad to simulate the body of a butterfly. On each plate, arrange 4 fish fillets to represent butterfly wings and 2 chives to represent antennae.

Makes 6 servings

■ Baked Rack of Lamb ■
with Bread Crumbs and Herbs
Carrè d'Agnello Gratinato alle Erbe

Serve with grilled tomatoes, and roast potatoes sprinkled with fresh thyme.

2 racks of lamb (about 2 lb/1 kg each), trimmed of fat

Salt to taste

2 tablespoons extra-virgin olive oil

¼ cup (2 oz/60 g) Dijon mustard

2 cups (2 oz/60 g) of mixed minced fresh thyme, sage, rosemary, and mint

1 cup (2 oz/60 g) fresh bread crumbs (see Basics)

Preheat the oven to 400°F (200°C).

Cut each rack of lamb in half; there will be 3 or 4 chops per half. Season with salt. Pour the olive oil into a roasting pan and add the lamb racks. Bake in the preheated oven for 15 minutes; remove from the oven.

Preheat the broiler. Brush the fat side of the racks with the mustard and sprinkle with the chopped herbs. Roll the lamb in the bread crumbs to coat thickly. Broil about 4 inches from the heat source until the crumbs are golden brown, about 5 minutes.

Makes 4 servings

VILLA SAN MICHELE

■ Orange Cream-Filled Charlottes ■
Piccola Charlotte all'Aurum

At Villa San Michele, these delectable cream-filled desserts are flavored with Aurum, an Italian orange liqueur. Other orange liqueurs, such as Grand Marnier, Cointreau, or Triple Sec, may be used instead.

Almond Cake

¾ cup (3 oz/90 g) almond flour*

7 tablespoons (3½ oz/105 g) sugar

2 eggs

4 egg whites

4 teaspoons melted butter

½ cup (5 oz/155 g) orange marmalade

Orange Cream

1 package plain gelatin

¼ cup (2 oz/60 ml) cold water

¾ cup (6 fl oz/180 ml) milk

2 egg yolks

6 tablespoons (3 oz/90 g) sugar

3 tablespoons Aurum or other orange liqueur

¾ cup (6 fl oz/180 ml) heavy (whipping) cream,
   beaten to stiff peaks

To make the cake: Preheat the oven to 475°F (245°C). Line the bottom of an 8-inch (20-cm) square baking pan with parchment paper and butter well. Dust with flour and knock out the excess.

In a blender or food processor, combine the almond flour, 6 tablespoons (3 oz/90 g) of the sugar, and one of the eggs and process until smooth. Add the other egg and process until smooth. Pour into a large bowl.

In a large bowl, beat the egg whites with the remaining 1 tablespoon of the sugar until stiff, glossy peaks form. Fold the egg whites and melted butter into the batter. Pour into the prepared pan and bake in the preheated oven for 6 to 7 minutes, or until a knife inserted in the center comes out clean. Let cool.

Cut the cake into 4 lengthwise slices. Spread orange marmalade on top of 3 slices. Stack the slices so the last is without marmalade. Cut into ¼-inch-thick (½-cm) slices. Line the bottom and sides of six 3-inch-diameter (7-cm) ramekins with the slices.

To make the cream: Sprinkle the gelatin over the water and let soak for 3 minutes. Meanwhile, in a small saucepan, bring the milk to a boil over medium-low heat.

In a large bowl, beat the egg yolks with the sugar. Gradually whisk in the hot milk. Stir in the gelatin mixture and let cool. Stir in the liqueur. Gently fold in the whipped cream. Divide the mixture among the ramekins and refrigerate at least 6 hours or up to 3 days.

To serve, run a knife around the inside edge of each mold and invert onto a plate.

Makes 6 servings

*Almond flour is available from The Baker's Catalog (see Resources).

CRISTOFORO MUNARI. Still Life with Musical Instruments and Fruit. Soprintendenza, Florence, Italy

VIVANDE

San Francisco, California

Born in Buffalo, New York, of Sicilian immigrant parents, Carlo Middione was the youngest of thirteen children. For generations his family on both sides were restaurateurs and innkeepers in Italy. Carlo received practical cooking training from his parents, who were both accomplished restaurant cooks. Before opening Vivande in 1995, Middione spent more than twenty years studying Italian cuisine, teaching Italian cooking classes, and writing award-winning cookbooks. Vivande (which means "things to live by") is located in Opera Plaza, just two blocks from the San Francisco opera, symphony, and ballet, near the city's historic Civic Center.

Middione established Vivande with a desire to offer exceptional cooking in a gracious atmophere devoid of stuffiness or pretension. His cooking is acclaimed for its integrity and elegant simplicity. Middione cherishes perfect ingredients, and their flavors are always allowed to shine through in his finished dishes. Since 1981, he has also run Vivande Porta Via, a popular European-style take-out food store and restaurant purveying Italian foods that are freshly made on the premises. In 1998, Middione received the prestigious Insegna del Ristorante Italiano del Mondo from the president of Italy for his achievement in the culinary arts and for being a goodwill ambassador for all things Italian.

One of the most beautiful dining rooms in San Francsico, Vivande is reminiscent of a Tuscan country villa filled with mementos, antiques, and art from all the regions of Italy. A team of talented artisans has created a room that juxtaposes stately and whimsical elements, from the commedia dell'arte figures painted on the walls to the stone sculpture of an open mouth that frames the restaurant's fifteen-foot front door (it was fashioned after one found on a building at the top of the Spanish Steps in Rome). The reception area is modeled after the Caffè Florian in Venice, and velvet banquettes and an antique Venetian glass chandelier light up the lounge. A glowing exhibition kitchen-with hand-painted Italian ceramics, a wood-fired pizza oven, and a wood-burning grill with a *girar-rosto* (roasting spit) is central to the main dining room. Chef Middione created the following menu and recipes for Menus and Music.

MENU

Baked Ricotta Cheese
Ricotta al Forno

Erice-Style Tomato Sauce
Salsa Ericina

Salmon in Parchment
Salmone in Cartoccio

Belgian Endive Salad
Insalata di Endivia Belga

Strawberries with Neapolitan Lemon Liqueur
Fragole al Limoncello

■ Baked Ricotta Cheese ■
Ricotta al Forno

Baked ricotta is sweet and moist inside and caramelized and dark on top. It can be made several days ahead and reheated when needed. Leftover baked ricotta will keep, covered with plastic wrap, for up to 1 week in the refrigerator.

15 ounces (470 g) whole-milk ricotta
  (preferably sheep's milk ricotta)

1 teaspoon sea salt

1 tablespoon coarsely ground pepper

Erice-Style Tomato Sauce for serving, (optional);
  recipe follows

8 to 12 bruschetta for serving (see Basics)

Put the ricotta in a cheesecloth-lined strainer over a container and let drain in the refrigerator for at least 4 hours or as long as overnight.

Preheat the oven to 450°F (230°C) for 10 minutes. Place an oven rack in the upper third of the oven. Line a pyramid- or dome-shaped mold (such as a deep bowl) with plastic wrap and spoon in the ricotta. To make individual baked ricottas, use mini-muffin cups lined with plastic wrap.

Unmold the ricotta by inverting it onto an ovenproof dish or pie pan. Sprinkle evenly with the salt and pepper. Let sit for about 10 minutes. Bake in the preheated oven for 20 minutes, or until the top of the ricotta is very dark, almost black. If not dark enough, raise the temperature to 500°F (260°C) and bake for another 5 minutes.

Let cool slightly. Pour the sauce around the ricotta, if using, and serve with bruschetta.

Makes about 1 pound (500 g); serves 4 to 6

■ Erice-Style Tomato Sauce ■
Salsa Ericina

Erice is perched on top of a mountain high above the city of Trapani on the southwest coast of Sicily. It is one of the most beautiful sites in Italy. This uncooked sauce is served at room temperature with baked ricotta, tossed with hot penne pasta, spread on bruschetta, or used as a sauce for hot or cold green beans. It is also delicious spooned over grilled fish or chicken, or hot or cold shrimp or lobster. Garnish with crumbled goat cheese if desired.

1½ pounds (750 g) Roma (plum) tomatoes, peeled and finely chopped (see Basics)

¼ cup (2 fl oz/60 ml) extra-virgin olive oil, or more to taste

Salt and freshly ground pepper to taste

½ cup (¾ oz/20 g) chopped fresh basil, or more to taste

⅓ cup (⅓ oz/10 g) chopped fresh flat-leaf parsley

1 tablespoon minced garlic, or to taste

In a large bowl, combine all the ingredients. Mix together and let rest for 1 hour or so. The sauce can be made ahead and refrigerated, but let it come to room temperature before using.

Makes about 2 cups

Beet Variation

Trim the roots from 4 large red beets, then trim the stems to about ¼ inch (6 mm). Scrub the beets well, then dry and rub them liberally with extra-virgin olive oil. Wrap the beets in aluminum foil or place in a small covered pan and bake in a preheated 375°F (190°C) oven for 1½ hours, or until tender when pierced with a knife. Let cool; peel and trim. Cut the beets into ¼-inch (6-mm) dice and use in place of the tomatoes in the above recipe.

■ Salmon in Parchment ■
Salmone in Cartoccio

The salmon is served sealed in packets so each person can open his or her serving at the table. Accompany with crusty bread.

¼ cup (2 fl oz/60 ml) extra-virgin olive oil

Six 6-ounce (185-g) salmon fillets, all the same shape

2 zucchini, cut into julienne

1 large carrot, peeled and cut into fine julienne

2 yellow crookneck squash, cut into ⅛-inch-thick (3-mm) diagonal slices

2 scallions, sliced ⅛ inch (3 mm) thick

Salt and freshly ground pepper to taste

12 large fresh basil leaves

24 thin slices English (hothouse) cucumber

3 lemons, halved and sliced into crowns (see Basics)

Preheat the oven to 375°F (190°C). Cut parchment paper into six 12-by-18-inch (30-by-45-cm) rectangles (don't use aluminum foil, or the salmon will overcook). Fold each rectangle in half to 9 by 12 inches (23 by 30 cm).

Open the parchment papers again and generously brush olive oil on the right half of each rectangle. Lay a salmon fillet on the oiled half of each rectangle very close to the fold and centered. Place one sixth of the zucchini, carrot, and squash around each salmon fillet. Scatter the scallions over, season with salt and pepper, and top each fillet with 2 basil leaves. Fold the open edges of the paper over several times to make a tight seal.

Place the packets close together on a baking sheet and bake in the preheated oven for 9 to 11 minutes, depending on the thickness of the fish, or until the salmon is opaque on the outside but still slightly translucent in the center. Place a packet on each of 6 hot plates, slightly off-center. Place a circle of 4 cucumber slices off to the side on each plate and place a lemon crown in the center. Serve immediately. Each person should open his or her packet by ripping open the top and eating out of the parchment. Serve with crusty bread.

Makes 6 servings

VIVANDE

■ Belgian Endive Salad ■
Insalata di Endivia Belga

Like many Italian salads, this one uses no vinegar or lemon juice, just plenty of extra-virgin olive oil and salt.

4 Belgian endives (mixed yellow and red if possible), or leaves from 1 large head raddicchio di Chioggia

⅔ cup (3 oz/90 g) coarsely chopped walnuts

1 cup (4 oz/125 g) Parmesan cheese shards (about the size of a hazelnut)

Salt and coarsely ground pepper to taste

¼ cup (2 fl oz/60 ml) extra-virgin olive oil, or to taste

1 white truffle, any size you can afford, sliced paper thin, or 2 tablespoons truffle purée, or 1 teaspoon white truffle oil

Slice the endives crosswise about 1 inch (2.5 cm) thick and separate them into rings. If using the raddicchio, tear the leaves into bit-sized pieces. Transfer to a large salad bowl. Add all the other ingredients and gently toss. Serve at room temperature with plenty of crusty Italian bread.

Makes 6 servings

■ Strawberries ■ with Neapolitan Lemon Liqueur
Fragole al Limoncello

If the strawberries are perfectly ripe, it may not necessary to use any sugar. If you wish, add up to 1 teaspoon coarsely ground black pepper and/or the grated zest of ½ lemon. Raspberries or blueberries may be used with or in place of the strawberries. Serve with crunchy cookies such as biscotti di Prato (see Basics) or plain sugar cookies.

2 cups (8 oz/250 g) fresh strawberries, hulled

3 tablespoons limoncello*

About 2 tablespoons sugar, or to taste

Slice the strawberries in half, or into thirds if they are very large, and place in a bowl. Add the limoncello and mix well. Add the sugar and mix well again. Set aside to macerate in the refrigerator for a couple of hours. Served chilled.

Makes 4 servings

*Limoncello is a sweet liqueur made from the peel of the lemons that grow in profusion and to an extraordinary size on the gorgeous Amalfi Coast.

CARAVAGGIO. Boy with a Basket of Fruit. Villa Borghese, Rome, Italy

VIVERE

Chicago, Illinois

Vivere (which means "to live" in Italian) is part of a three-restaurant complex housed in a village-like setting in Chicago's bustling Loop, the historic heart of the city's business district. Built in 1927 by Alfredo Capitanini, the restaurants have thrived under the stewardship of three generations of the Capitanini family. Gina, Alfredo, and Frank Capitanini, Jr., established Vivere in 1990 and operate it on a daily basis with input from Ray and Frank Capitanini, Sr. The restaurant serves superb regional Italian cuisine in a fanciful "contemporary Baroque" setting.

Vivere replaces the Capitanini's landmark Florentine Room, Chicago's oldest fine-dining Italian restaurant. Because of the Florentine Room's history of hosting opera performers and their fans, designer Jordan Mozer has used eclectic theatrical elements to create a fantastic, lively atmosphere. His design, including swagged silk draperies, sculptured wrought-iron stair rails, hand-blown conical glass light fixtures, curving woodwork, and floor-to-ceiling copper helixes, provides a festive setting in which to enjoy a leisurely meal.

Vivere's menu reflects the taste and refinement of chef Marcelo Gallegos. A native of Chicago, Gallegos worked with chef Paul Bartolotta at Chicago's Spiaggia restaurant and trained at the acclaimed Dal Pescatore in Italy's Lombardy region and Ristorante Locanda dell'Amorosa in Siena. Vivere hosts wine dinners throughout the year, and its wine cellar, one of the finest in the United States, boasts more than thirty thousand bottles carefully selected by proprietor Ray Capitanini and wine consultant Robert Rohden. Since 1984, their wine list has yearly received the Grand Award of Excellence from *Wine Spectator* magazine. The following dinner was created by chef Marcelo Gallegos, and the Raspberry and Brown Butter Tart was created by pastry chef Mary McMahon.

MENU

Tuscan Bread Salad
Panzanella

Little Agnolotti Stuffed with Pheasant
Agnolottini di Fagiano

Duck Breast with Sweet Balsamic Vinegar Sauce
Petto d'Anatra con Salsa d'Aceto Balsamico Dolce

Raspberry and Brown Butter Tart

Caeta, citron-candies without end;
And each shall drink and help his neighbor too.
And let the cold be great, and the fire grand:
And still for fowls, and pastries sweetly wrought,
For hares and kids, for roast and boiled, be sure
You always have your appetites at hand;

—Folgore da San Geminiano,
from "Of the Months: Twelve Sonnets
Addressed to a Fellowship of Sienese Nobles"

▪ Tuscan Bread Salad ▪

Panzanella

A brightly colored summer salad with ripe, intriguing flavors. Ciabatta is a flat, slipper-shaped bread with an airy texture inside and a pale, crisp crust. Any firm-textured Italian or French bread may be used.

1 day-old ciabatta loaf, crust trimmed, cut into ¾-inch (2-cm) dice

2 to 3 medium tomatoes, or 5 to 6 Roma (plum) tomatoes (12 oz/375 g total), peeled and halved (see Basics)

1 garlic clove crushed to a paste with a little salt

Salt and freshly ground pepper to taste

⅓ cup (3 fl oz/80 ml) extra-virgin olive oil, plus more for drizzling

4 teaspoons red wine vinegar

2 tablespoons capers

¼ cup (1 oz/30 g) pitted brine-cured black olives

1 *each* red and yellow bell pepper, roasted, peeled, and cut into 8 strips (see Basics)

3 anchovy fillets, chopped

½ cup (¾ oz/20 g) chopped fresh basil leaves

Put all the bread in a large bowl. Seed the tomatoes over a fine-meshed sieve set over a bowl to retain the juice. Stir in the garlic paste, salt, and pepper. Whisk in the ⅓ cup (3 fl oz/90 ml) olive oil and 3 teaspoons of the red wine vinegar. Pour over the bread and toss until all the liquid is absorbed. (Depending on how stale the bread is, more liquid may be required to soak the bread; if so, add more olive oil.)

In a small bowl, soak the capers in the remaining 1 teaspoon red wine vinegar; drain. Mix the bell pepper strips together.

In a serving bowl, arrange a layer of one-third of the soaked bread. Top with one-third of the mixed bell peppers, and one-third of the tomatoes. Sprinkle with capers, anchovies, olives, and basil. Repeat to make 2 more layers. Set the salad aside at room temperature for at least 1 hour before serving. Serve with extra-virgin olive oil to drizzle on at the table.

Makes 4 to 6 servings

■ Little Agnolotti ■ Stuffed with Pheasant
Agnolottini di Fagiano

At Vivere, these plump little pasta squares are lightly dressed with sage butter and filled with a flavorful mixture of braised pheasant, Parmesan cheese, and vegetables. Order pheasant from a specialty butcher shop, or use chicken instead.

Filling

2 tablespoons olive oil

1 onion, minced

2 tablespoons minced garlic

3 celery stalks, finely diced

2 carrots, peeled and finely diced

2 pounds (1 kg) boned pheasant legs or boned chicken thighs

2 cups (16 fl oz/500 ml) chicken broth (see Basics) or canned low-salt chicken broth

1 tablespoon chopped fresh flat-leaf (Italian) parsley

2 eggs, lightly beaten

½ cup (2 oz/60 g) freshly grated Parmesan cheese

Pinch of salt

Freshly ground pepper to taste

Pasta

2½ cups (12½ oz/390 g) all-purpose flour, plus more as needed

3 eggs

¼ teaspoon salt

Sage Butter

2 tablespoons butter

2 tablespoons clarified butter (see Basics)

10 fresh sage leaves

Salt and freshly ground pepper to taste

To make the filling: In a large sauté pan or skillet over medium heat, heat the olive oil and sauté the onion for 3 minutes. Add the garlic and sauté until fragrant. Add the celery and carrots and sauté until soft, about 5 minutes. Cut each pheasant leg, if using, into 4 pieces. Cut the chicken thighs, if using, in half. Add the pheasant or chicken to the pan. Add the broth and simmer for 30 minutes, or until very tender. Transfer to a medium bowl and let cool. Transfer to a food processor and pulse until smooth, or pass through a fine-holed meat grinder. Stir in the parsley, eggs, Parmesan cheese, salt, and pepper.

To make the pasta: Pour the 2½ cups (12½ oz/390 g) flour into a mound on a work surface and make a well in the center. Add the eggs and salt to the well, and using a fork, beat just until blended. Begin mixing the flour into the egg mixture, drawing the flour from the inside wall of the well until a dough is formed. Alternatively, add the flour, eggs, and salt to the bowl of a food processor and process until the mixture just forms a ball. If the dough is sticky, add a little more flour, to make a smooth dough.

On a floured work surface, knead the dough for 8 minutes, or until smooth and elastic. Cut the dough into 4 equal sections, enclose in plastic wrap, and let rest at least 10 minutes before rolling out.

Set the rollers of a pasta machine at the highest number. Flatten one piece of dough into a rough rectangle and feed it through the rollers. Fold in half and feed through the rollers 8 or 9 more times, folding the dough in half each time and dusting with flour if necessary to prevent sticking. Turn the dial down one notch and feed the dough through the rollers without folding. Continue feeding the dough through the rollers without folding, turning the dial one notch lower each time until the second-lowest notch is reached. The dough will be a smooth long sheet, 4 to 5 inches (10 to 13 cm) wide.

Place ½ teaspoon of the filling at 1½-inch (4-cm) intervals over half a sheet of dough. Fold the dough over to cover the filling, pressing with the fingers around each mound. Using a fluted pastry wheel, cut between the 2-inch (5-cm) squares. Place on a flour-dusted cookie sheet until time to cook; they can dry an hour or so before cooking.

In a large pot of salted boiling water, cook the agnolotti until they float to the top, about 3 minutes; drain.

To make the sage butter: In a large sauté pan or skillet combine the butter, clarified butter, sage, salt, and pepper. Cook over low heat until the butter starts to melt. Turn off heat. Add the pasta, lightly toss, and serve hot.

Makes 6 servings

■ Duck Breast ■
with Sweet Balsamic Vinegar Sauce

Petto d'Anatra con Salsa d'Aceto Balsamico Dolce

The flavor of duck is complemented by this fruity, slightly acidic sauce.

¾ cup (6 fl oz/185 ml) dry red wine

½ cup (4 oz/125 g) sugar

2 pears, peeled, cored, and diced

6 tablespoons (3 fl oz/80 ml) veal demi-glace,* or reduced veal or
  beef broth (see Basics)

2½ tablespoons balsamic vinegar

6 duck breasts, 8 ounces (250 g) each**

Salt and freshly ground pepper to taste

In a medium saucepan, bring the wine and sugar to a boil over high heat. Add the pears and cook to reduce the liquid by three fourths. Strain the mixture through a fine-meshed sieve, pushing the solids through with the back of a spoon. Alternatively, transfer the mixture to a food processor and purée until smooth.

In a medium saucepan, combine the red wine mixture, demi-glace or broth, balsamic vinegar, salt, and pepper and cook until reduced to a thick saucelike consistency; set aside.

Score a crisscross pattern in the skin of the duck breasts with a sharp knife. Sprinkle with salt and pepper.

Heat 2 large sauté pans or skillets over medium-high heat until very hot. Add the duck breasts, skin-side down, cook until golden brown, about 10 minutes. Pour off the fat, reduce heat to medium, and turn the breasts over; cook for 5 minutes for medium rare. Remove the duck from the pan and let rest for 30 seconds so the juices flow through the meat. Slice the breasts and fan each out onto a plate. Spoon the sauce over and serve immediately.

Makes 6 servings

*Veal demi-glace, a super-concentrated stock, adds magnificent flavor. Preparation from scratch takes hours, but it is available by mail order (see Resources).

**Frozen duck breasts are available in many supermarkets, or see Resources.

■ Raspberry and Brown Butter Tart ■

Pasta frolla, a sweet, buttery pastry dough, is the basis of many Italian desserts.

Pasta Frolla

¾ cup (6 oz/185 g) butter at room temperature

¾ cup (6 oz/185 g) sugar

1 egg

1 egg yolk

1 teaspoon vanilla extract

2 cups (10 oz/315 g) all-purpose flour

½ teaspoon salt

Raspberry Filling

3 eggs

1 cup (8 oz/250 g) sugar

½ cup (2½ oz/75 g) all-purpose flour

¾ cup (6 oz/185 g) butter

1 vanilla bean, split lengthwise, or 1 teaspoon vanilla extract

1 cup (4 oz/125 g) fresh raspberries

Topping

½ cup (5 oz/155 g) apricot jam

2 cups (8 oz/250 g) fresh raspberries

To make the pasta frolla: In a large bowl, beat the butter and sugar together until light and fluffy. Beat in the egg, egg yolk, and vanilla. Stir in the flour and salt to form a soft dough. Shape the dough into a ball, cover with plastic wrap, and refrigerate for at least 2 hours.

Preheat the oven to 350°F (180°C). On a lightly floured work surface, roll the dough out into a 12-inch-diameter (30-cm) circle. Fit the dough into a 10-inch (25-cm) tart pan with a removable bottom and press gently in place; trim the edges by running the rolling pin around the top of the pan.

VIVERE

To make the filling: In a medium bowl, whisk the eggs, sugar, and flour together until smooth; set aside.

In a heavy saucepan or skillet over medium heat, melt the butter. Add the vanilla bean, if using, and cook until the butter foams. Continue heating until the butter browns and gives off a nutty aroma. Remove from heat and remove the vanilla bean, if using. Gradually whisk the butter mixture into the egg mixture. Stir in the vanilla extract, if using.

Arrange the berries in the bottom of the pastry-lined tart pan. Pour in the butter mixture. Bake in the preheated oven for 45 minutes to 1 hour, or until the crust is golden brown. Let cool.

In a small, heavy saucepan, bring the apricot jam to a boil over medium-high heat, stirring constantly. Push through a fine-meshed sieve with the back of a spoon. Brush the top of the tart with the sieved jam. Cover with a layer of raspberries. Unmold the tart and serve.

Makes 8 to 10 servings

BASICS

Almond Biscotti Biscotti di Prato

2¼ cups (11½ oz/360 g) all-purpose flour

¾ cup (6 oz/185 g) sugar

1½ teaspoons baking powder

¼ teaspoon salt

3 eggs, beaten lightly

⅔ cup (4 oz/125 g) unblanched almonds, chopped

Preheat the oven to 400°F (200°C). Grease and flour a baking sheet, or line it with parchment paper.

In a medium bowl, stir the flour, sugar, baking powder, and salt together. Stir in the eggs to form a smooth, stiff dough. Knead in the almonds.

On a lightly floured board, divide the dough into 4 parts and shape into 4 logs about 1 inch (2.5 cm) thick. Place on the prepared baking sheet, spacing the logs at least 2 inches (5 cm) apart.

Bake in the preheated oven until golden brown, about 30 minutes. Transfer from the baking sheet to a wire rack and let cool for 5 minutes. Using a serrated knife, cut the logs diagonally (at a 45 degree angle) into ½-inch-thick (12-mm) slices. Lay the slices, cut-side up, on the prepared pan and bake for 5 minutes. Turn the biscotti over and bake for 5 minutes. Let cool completely on wire racks. Store in an airtight container.

Makes about 40 cookies

Bruschetta

The word bruschetta comes from bruscare, which means "to roast over coals" in Italian, the original and still the best way of toasting bread. Traditionally served before a meal, bruschetta show off good-quality extra-virgin olive oil. They can be served plain, with slices of ripe tomato and a few fresh basil leaves, or with other toppings or spreads.

12 slices Italian bread ½ to ¾ inch (12 mm to 2 cm) thick

6 garlic cloves, halved

12 tablespoons (6 fl oz/180 ml) extra-virgin olive oil

Salt and freshly ground black pepper to taste

Toast the bread over hot coals or under a preheated broiler on both sides until golden; the bread should be crisp around the edges and slightly soft in the center. While still hot, rub one side of each toast with the cut side of a garlic clove. Arrange on a platter, garlic-rubbed side up, and drizzle 1 tablespoon olive oil over each toast. Sprinkle with salt and pepper. Serve immediately.

Makes 12 bruschetta

Candied Orange Peel

2 oranges, scrubbed

¾ cup (6 oz/185 g) sugar

1 cup (8 fl oz/250 ml) water

Using a sharp knife, cut the peel off the top and bottom of the oranges down to the flesh. Standing the oranges on one cut end, cut off 2-inch (5-cm) strips of zest (the orange part only) from top to bottom. Cut the strips in half lengthwise. Cut the strips in half again to ½ inch (12 mm) wide.

    In a small, heavy saucepan, combine the sugar and water and bring to a boil over medium heat. Add the strips of orange peel and simmer gently for 10 minutes. Remove from heat and let cool in the syrup. Store in an airtight container.

Makes about 1 cup (6 oz/185 g)

Clarified Butter

Clarified butter is used for cooking at high temperatures, as it will not burn. In a small, heavy saucepan, melt unsalted butter over low heat. Remove the pan from heat and let stand for several minutes. Skim off the foam and pour off the clear liquid, leaving the milk solids in the bottom of the pan. Cover and store in the refrigerator indefinitely. When clarified, butter loses about one fourth its original volume.

Crostini

Small enough to eat in one or two bites, these "little toasts" are served as a basic for Italian antipasti. There are hundreds of choices for crostini toppings, as long as they are neat and compact so they don't fall off.

1 day-old Italian or French baguette (not sourdough)
Extra-virign olive oil for brushing

Preheat the oven to 375°F (190°C). Cut the bread into ¼-inch-thick (6-mm) slices. Brush lightly with the olive oil. Arrange the bread on a baking sheet and bake in the preheated oven for about 10 mintues, or until lightly golden; let cool. Store in an airtight container.

Makes 36 to 40 toasts

Beef Broth Brodo di Carne

Italian beef broth is less concentrated in flavor than beef stock, because Italians don't roast the bones first, as the French do.

5 pounds (2.5 kg) assorted beef short ribs and veal breast and rib bones
2 carrots, peeled and chopped
2 celery stalks, chopped
1 onion, chopped
1 tomato, chopped
1 flat-leaf (Italian) parsley sprig
1 tablespoon black peppercorns
1 teaspoon salt (optional)

In a large stockpot, combine all the ingredients and add enough water to cover by 2 inches (5 cm). Bring to a boil over high heat. Skim off any foam that rises to the surface. Reduce heat to low and simmer, uncovered, for about 3 hours, or until well flavored. Strain through a fine-meshed sieve and let cool. Refrigerate overnight, then remove and discard the congealed fat on top. Store, covered, in the refrigerator for up to 3 days. To keep longer, bring to a boil every 3 days, or freeze for up to 3 months

Makes about 8 cups (64 fl oz/2 l)

Chicken Broth Brodo di Pollo

One 3-pound (1.5 kg) chicken
1 celery stalk
1 onion
1 carrot
1 tomato
1 teaspoon salt (optional)
1 teaspoon black peppercorns
3 quarts cold water

In a large stockpot, combine all the ingredients and add enough water to cover by 2 inches (5 cm). Bring to a boil over high heat. Skim off any foam that rises to the surface. Reduce heat to low and simmer, uncovered, for about 3 hours, or until well flavored. Strain through a fine-meshed sieve and let cool, uncovered. Refrigerate overnight, then remove and discard the congealed fat on top. Store covered in the refrigerator for up to 3 days. To keep longer, bring to a boil every 3 days, or freeze for up to 3 months.

Put the chicken meat through the meat grinder to use as pasta filling.

Makes about 8 cups (64 fl oz/2 l)

Fish Stock

12 ounces (375 g) fish bones and scraps from mild-tasting fish like
  red snapper
1 onion
1 celery stalk
3 thyme sprigs
2 bay leaves
3 flat-leaf (Italian) parsley sprigs
1 teaspoon white peppercorns
½ cup (4 fl oz/125 ml) dry white wine
2 teaspoons salt (optional)
8 cups water (64 fl oz/2 l)

BASICS

In a large pot, combine all the ingredients and bring to a boil. Reduce heat to low and simmer, uncovered, for 45 minutes, skimming any foam that rises to the surface. Strain through a fine-meshed sieve, pressing on the solids with the back of a large spoon to extract their juices. Let cool. Cover and refrigerate for up to 2 days. To keep longer, bring to a boil every 2 days, or freeze up to 2 months.

Makes about 8 cups (64 fl oz/2 l)

Fried Zucchini Blossoms Fiori di Zucchine Fritti

If you grow zucchini in your garden, use the bright yellow-orange blossoms in this classic summer dish. Try to pick only male flowers that are still firmly closed. (The female flowers, which go on to produce the vegetables, have thicker stems than the males).

12 to 16 tightly closed zucchini blossoms, washed and dried

1 cup (8 fl oz/250 ml) water

Vegetable oil for deep-frying

¾ cup (4 oz/125 g) all-purpose flour

Salt and freshly ground pepper to taste

Cut the base of the blossoms on one side and open the flower flat.
    Pour the water into a small bowl. Gradually sift in the flour, while beating constantly with a fork; the batter will be quite thick.
    In a large sauté pan or skillet over high heat, heat the olive oil until the surface shimmers. Dip the blossoms in the batter and slip them into the hot oil. Deep-fry until golden brown on all sides. Using a slotted spoon, transfer to paper towels to drain. Sprinkle with salt and pepper and serve immediately.

Oil and Vinegar Dressing

Pinch of salt

2 tablespoons red wine vinegar

½ cup (4 fl oz/125 ml) extra-virgin olive oil

In a small bowl, combine the salt and vinegar and stir to dissolve the salt. Sprinkle over the salad. Pour over the olive oil and toss until very well mixed. Serve immediately.

Makes about ½ cup (4 fl oz/125 ml)

Ladyfingers Savoiardi

½ cup (4 oz/125 g) plus 1 tablespoon granulated sugar

3 eggs, separated

1 teaspoon vanilla extract

Pinch of salt

½ teaspoon cream of tartar

⅔ cup (4 oz/125 g) all-purpose flour

1 cup (4 oz/125 g) powdered sugar for dusting

Preheat the oven to 325°F (165°C). Butter 2 baking sheets and dust lightly with flour; knock off any excess.

In a large bowl, beat the ½ cup (4 oz/125 g) sugar, the egg yolks, and vanilla together until pale and the mixture forms a slowly dissolving ribbon on the surface when a beater is lifted, about 3 minutes.

In a large bowl, beat the egg whites until foamy. Beat in the salt and cream of tartar until soft peaks form. Sprinkle in the 1 tablespoon granulated sugar and beat until stiff, glossy peaks form. Stir one fourth of the egg white mixture into the egg yolk mixture. Sprinkle one fourth of the flour over the top of this mixture and fold it in until partially blended. Fold in half the remaining egg whites until blended, then half of the remaining flour. Repeat with the remaining whites and flour until blended. The batter should be light and fluffy.

Using a pastry bag, make even lines of batter 4 inches (10 cm) long and ¾ inch (2 cm) wide on the prepared baking sheets. Dust the cookies with the powdered sugar. Bake immediately in the preheated oven for 20 minutes, or until the ladyfingers are very pale brown under their sugar coating. Transfer the cookies to wire racks and let cool.

Makes about 25 ladyfingers

Leek Frizzles

These frizzles give dishes a glamorous look and some sweet crunch.

Cut a 2 inch (5 cm) piece of the white part of a leek in half lengthwise. Separate each into 3 or 4 layers and slice these thinly. Repeat to cut the remaining pieces. In a medium skillet, heat ½ inch (12 mm) oil over medium-high heat, until the surface shimmers. Add the leek pieces and cook until they begin to brown. Using a slotted spoon, transfer to paper towels to drain. Keep at room temperature until ready to use.

Makes about ½ cup

Lemon and Orange Zest

To make strips: Using a vegetable peeler or sharp paring knife, cut thin strips of the colored part (the zest) of the lemon or orange peel; don't include the white pith underneath, which is apt to be bitter. To grate: Use a grater or zester to remove the zest of the lemon or orange.

Peeling and Seeding Tomatoes

Cut out the cores of the tomatoes and cut an X in the opposite end. Drop the tomatoes into a pot of rapidly bvoiling water for 10 seconds, or until the skin by the X peels away slightly. Drain and run cold water over the tomatoes; the skin should slip off easily. To seed, cut the tomatoes in half crosswise, hold each half upside down over the sink (or a fine-meshed sieve over a bowl, if you want to save the juice), and gently squeeze and shake to remove the seeds.

Reduced Broth

Simmer broth over medium heat until reduced by about one third, or until richly flavored.

Roasting Peppers

Char whole peppers over a gas flame, turning to blacken the skin all over. Or, cut the peppers into fourths, core, seed, and derib. Place on a broiler pan lined with aluminum foil. Press to flatten slightly and char under a preheated broiler until blackened. Using tongs, transfer the peppers to a paper or plastic bag, close it, and let the peppers cool for 10 to 15 minutes. Remove from the bag, peel off the skin with your fingers or a small sharp knife.

To Section Citrus Fruit

Cut off the top and bottom of an orange, grapefruit, lime, or lemon down to the flesh, then stand the fruit upright. Using a large, sharp knife, cut off the peel in sections down to the flesh. Working over a bowl to catch the juice and segments, hold the fruit in one hand and cut out each segment by slicing between the flesh and each side of each membrane.

Sponge Cake

6 eggs, separated

1 cup (8 oz/250 g) sugar

1 cup (5 oz/155 g) all-purpose flour

½ (4 oz/125 g) butter, melted

Pinch of salt

Preheat the oven to 350°F (180°C). Line a 14-by-11-inch rimmed baking sheet (jelly roll pan) with parchment paper.

Using an electric mixer, beat the egg yolks and ½ cup (4 oz/125 g) of the sugar until pale and the mixture forms a slowly dissolving ribbon on the surface when a beater is lifted, about 3 minutes.

In another bowl and with a clean beater, beat the egg whites until soft peaks form. Add the remaining ½ cup (4 oz/125 g) sugar and beat until stiff, glossy peaks form. Gently fold the egg whites into the yolk mixture. Sift the flour and salt over the top of the egg mixture and fold it in. Dribble the butter over the batter and fold it in until blended.

Spread the batter evenly in the prepared pan. Bake in the preheated oven for 14 minutes, or until a skewer inserted in the center comes out clean. Let cool for 5 minutes. Run a knife around the edge of the cake and invert it onto a cooling rack. Peel off the parchment and let the cake cool completely.

Toasting Almonds and Walnuts

Preheat the oven to 350°F (180°C). Spread the nuts on a baking sheet and bake, stirring once or twice, for 5 to 10 minutes, or until fragrant and very lightly browned.

Toasting and Skinning Hazelnuts

Preheat the oven to 350°F (180°C). Spread the nuts on a baking sheet and bake, stirring once or twice, for 10 to 15 minutes or until lightly browned. Remove from the oven, fold in a kitchen towel, and rub the hazelnuts with the towel to remove the skins. Pour the nuts into a colander and shake it over the sink to discard the remaining skins.

Conversion Charts

Weight Measurements

Standard U.S.	Ounces	Metric
1 ounce	1	30 g
1/4 pound	4	125 g
1/2 pound	8	250 g
1 pound	16	500 g
1 1/2 pounds	24	750 g
2 pounds	32	1 kg
2 1/2 pounds	40	1.25 kg
3 pounds	48	1.5 kg

Volume Measurements

Standard U.S.	Fluid Ounces	Metric
1 tablespoon	1/2	15 ml
2 tablespoons	1	30 ml
3 tablespoons	1 1/2	45 ml
1/4 cup (4 tablespoons)	2	60 ml
6 tablespoons	3	90 ml
1/2 cup (8 tablespoons)	4	125 ml
1 cup	8	250 ml
1 pint (2 cups)	16	500 ml
4 cups	32	1 l

Oven Temperatures

Fahrenheit	Celsius	Gas Mark
250°	120°	1/2
275°	135°	1
300°	150°	2
325°	165°	3
350°	180°	4
375°	190°	5
400°	200°	6
425°	220°	7

Note: For ease of use, measurements have been rounded off.

Conversion Factors

Ounces to grams: Multiply the ounce figure by 28.3 to get the number of grams.

Pounds to grams: Multiply the pound figure by 453.59 to get the number of grams.

Pounds to kilograms: Multiply the pound figure by 0.45 to get the number of kilograms.

Ounces to milliliters: Multiply the ounce figure by 30 to get the number of milliliters.

Cups to liters: Multiply the cup figure by 0.24 to get the number of liters.

Fahrenheit to Celsius: Subtract 32 from the Fahrenheit figure, multiply by 5, then divide by 9 to get the Celsius figure.

Contributors

Acquerello

1722 Sacramento Street
San Francisco, CA 94109 U.S.A.
Phone: (415) 567-5432

Il Bottaccio

Via Bottaccio, 1
54038 Montignoso, Italy
Phone: 39 0585 34 00 31
Fax: 39 0585 34 01 03

Hotel Certosa di Maggiano

Strada di Certosa, 82
53100 Siena, Italy
Phone: 39 0577 28 81 80
Fax: 39 0577 28 81 89

Hotel Cipriani

Giudecca, 10
30133 Venice, Italy
Phone: 39 41 520 77 44
Fax: 39 41 520 77 45

Don Alfonso 1890

Corso Sant'Agata, 11
80064 Sant'Agata sui Due Golfi
(Naples) Italy
Phone: 39 081 878 00 26
Fax: 39 081 533 02 26

Galileo

1110 Twenty-first Street NW
Washington, D.C. 20036 U.S.A.
Phone: (202) 293-7191

Genoa

2832 Southeast Belmont Street
Portland, OR 97214 U.S.A.
Phone: (503) 238-1464

Mi Piaci

14854 Montfort
Dallas, TX 75240 U.S.A.
Phone: (972) 934-8424

Remi

1325 Avenue of the Americas
New York, NY 10019 U.S.A.
Phone: (212) 581-4242

San Domenico NY

240 Central Park South
New York, NY 10019 U.S.A.
Phone: (212) 265-5959

Il Sole di Ranco

Piazza Venezia, 5
21020 Ranco (Varese), Italy
Phone: 39 0331 97 65 07
Fax: 39 0331 97 66 20

Sotto Sotto

313 N. Highland Avenue
Atlanta, GA 30307 U.S.A.
Phone: (404) 523-6678

Spiaggia

1 Magnificent Mile
980 North Michigan
Chicago, IL 60611 U.S.A.
Phone: (312) 280-2750

Il Terrazzo Carmine
411 First Avenue South
Seattle, WA 98104 U.S.A.
Phone: (206) 467-7797

Va Pensiero Restaurant
1500 Oak Avenue
Evanston, IL 60201 U.S.A.
Phone: (847) 475-7779

Valentino
3115 Pico Boulevard
Santa Monica, CA 90405 U.S.A.
Phone: (310) 829-4313

Hotel Villa Cipriani
Via Canova, 298
31011 Asolo (Treviso), Italy
Phone: 39 0423 523411
Fax: 39 0423 952095

Villa del Lupo
869 Hamilton Street
Vancouver, British Columbia
V6B 2R7 Canada
Phone: (604) 688-7436

Villa San Michele
Via Doccia, 4
50014 Fiesole (Florence), Italy
Phone: 39 55 59451
Fax: 39 55 598734

Vivande Ristorante
670 Golden Gate
San Francisco, CA 94102 U.S.A.
Phone: (415) 673-9245

Vivere
71 West Monroe Street
Chicago, IL 60603 U.S.A.
Phone: (312) 332-4040

CONTRIBUTORS

Resources

The Baker's Catalogue King Arthur's Flour

P.O. Box 876
Norwich, VT 05055-0876
(800) 827-6836
www.kingarthurflour.com

Hazelnut paste, pasta flour, chestnut and almond flour, bitter almond oil, candied citron peel, and sparkling colored sugars.

Balducci's

95 Sherwood Avenue
Farmingdale, NY 11735
(800) 225-3822
www.balducci.com

Olives, prosciutto, Italian cheeses, salami, sausages, lobster, breads, biscotti, truffles, truffle oil, demi-glace.

Corti Brothers Grocers & Wine Merchants

P.O. Box 191358
5810 Folsom Boulevard
Sacramento, CA 95819
(916) 736-3800

Olive oils, vinegars, pasta, dried fish, wine, olives, dried mushrooms and vegetables.

Dean & DeLuca, Catalog Center

2526 East 36th Street, North Circle
Wichita, KS 67219
(800) 221-7714
www.deandeluca.com

Smoked salmon, sausages, salami, Italian cheeses, espresso, chocolate, spices, pasta, sardines, anchovies, truffles, truffle oil, balsamic vinegar, olive oil.

Di Palo Fine Foods

206 Grand Street
New York, NY 10013
(212) 226-1033

Italian cheeses, vinegars, olive oil, balsamic vinegar.

Polarica

105 Quince Street
San Francisco, CA 94124
(800) 426-3872
www.polarica.com

Rabbit, duck breast, pancetta, smoked salmon, caviar, truffles, sausages, squab, duck, guinea fowl.

Sur La Table Catalog Department

1765 Sixth Avenue South
Seattle, WA 98134
(800) 243-0852
www.surlatable.com

A selection of basic tools and equipment, as well as an assortment of hard-to-find specialty items for cooking and baking.

Todaro Brothers

555 Second Avenue
New York, NY 10016
(877) 472-2767

Cheeses, salami, sausages, olives, balsamic vinegars, dried mushrooms, truffles, dried beans, rice, olive oils, pasta, Italian pastries.

Urbani Truffles USA

2924 40th Avenue
Long Island City, NY 11101
(800) 281-2330
www.urbani.com

White Alba truffles, black truffles, truffle oil, truffle purée, truffle butter, mushrooms, caviar, smoked fish.

Williams-Sonoma

P.O. Box 379900
Las Vegas, NV 89137
(800) 541-2233
www.williams-sonoma.com

A wide variety of cooking supplies, dinnerware, glassware, table linens, and flatware; terrines and ramekins, candied citrus peel, demi-glace, and other specialty foods.

Zabars

2245 Broadway
New York, NY 10024
(800) 697-6301
www.zabars.com

Coffee beans, smoked salmon, Italian cheese, prosciutto, salami, balsamic vinegars, olive oils, amaretti.

Zingerman's Delicatessan

422 Detroit Street
Ann Arbor, MI 48104
(888) 636-8162
www.zingermans.com

Olive oil, balsamic vinegar, Italian cheeses, baked goods.

Acknowledgements

I would like to thank the many people who made this volume possible.

My deepest gratitude to the proprietors and chefs of the restaurants who generously contributed menus and recipes: Suzette Gresham-Tognetti, Giancarlo Paterlini, Nino Mosca, Kristin Sharpe, Elizabeth and Stefano D'Anna, Margherita Grossi, Anna Recordati, Natale Rusconi, Renato Piccolotto, Alfonso and Livia Iaccarino, Emanuel Weyringer, Roberto Donna, Catherine Whims, Kerry DeBuse, Phil and Janet Cobb, Kevin Ascolese, Francesco Antonucci, Adam D. Tihany, Tony May, Marisa May, Odette Fada, Carlo and Itala Brovelli, Davide Brovelli, Riccardo Ullio, Paul Bartolotta, Carmine Esmeraldo, Peggy Ryan, Piero Selvaggio, Angelo Auriana, Giampaolo Burattin, Secondo Ceccato, Chris Riley, Julio Gonzalez-Perini, Maurizio Saccani, Vittorio Dall'Ò, Attilio Fabrizio, Carlo and Lisa Middione, the Capitanini family, and Marcelo Gallegos.

Affectionate thanks to clarinetist Ken Peplowski, guitarist Bucky Pizzarelli, violinist Federico Britos, mandolinist Lou Pallo, bassist Greg Cohen, and accordionist Charlie Giordano. Thank you, Malcolm Addey, assisted by Scott Young, for the excellent recording done at Avatar Studios, New York City. Once again, I am most grateful to clarinetist Ken Peplowski for making the recording a dream come true.

Thank you to Augusto Marchini and the Italian Trade Commission, New York City, for the food and wine map of Italy; to Tony Kaye, whose mandolin appears on the cover; to Daniela Cossali for recipe translations; to Meg Shore for the translation of the Epicuro quote; and to Michael Bentley for a most memorable dinner.

My sincere thanks to Paul Moore for his beautiful photographs, to Amy Nathan for her stellar food styling, and to Sara Salvin for her stylish tableware.

Once again, deep gratitude to my longtime editor Carolyn Miller for her expert advice, editorial guidance, and attention to detail. And special thanks to Sarah Creider for her invaluable assistance during each phase of this entire project. Thanks to Brent Beck of Fifth Street Design for his book and cover design and his enthusiastic support of this project. I also owe many thanks to Sharilyn Hovind, Chelsea Shriver, Sharlene Swacke, Connie

Woods, Ned Waring, Tim Forney, Hugo Reichmuth, Erick Villatoro, Jesus Alcala, Jose Alcala, and all of the staff at Menus and Music.

And as always, to my daughters, Claire and Caitlin, and my husband, John, for their adventurous appetites and their love.

Photographic Credits: Alinari/Art Resource, NY: 32, 40, 50, 110, 177. Erich Lessing/Art Resource, NY: 62, 82. Nimatallah/Art Resource, NY: 18. Scala/Art Resource, NY: 1, 70, 100, 120, 140, 158, 168, 187, 206, 215.

Index